BREAKING *the* MEDICINE MONOPOLIES

Reflections of a Generic Drug Pioneer

ALFRED ENGELBERG

A POST HILL PRESS BOOK
ISBN: 979-8-88845-672-9
ISBN (eBook): 979-8-88845-673-6

Breaking the Medicine Monopolies:
Reflections of a Generic Drug Pioneer

Cover design by Cody Corcoran

This book contains advice and information relating to health care. It should be used to supplement rather than replace the advice of your doctor or another trained health professional. You are advised to consult your health professional with regard to matters related to your health, and in particular regarding matters that may require diagnosis or medical attention. All efforts have been made to assure the accuracy of the information in this book as of the date of publication. The publisher and the author disclaim liability for any medical outcomes that may occur as a result of applying the methods suggested in this book.

This is a work of nonfiction. All people, locations, events, and situations are portrayed to the best of the author's memory.

Post Hill Press
New York • Nashville
posthillpress.com

Published in the United States of America
1 2 3 4 5 6 7 8 9 10

To my mother, Gusti, who sacrificed everything
so I could live the American dream
and gave me the moral compass
to live it responsibly.

Table of Contents

Preface

I WAS A YOUNG PARTNER in a small intellectual property law firm when I got my first generic drug client in the mid-1970s. Premo Pharmaceutical, a family-run generic drug business, hired me to defend a claim that they infringed Upjohn's patent on Orinase, a pill for treating diabetes. It was a turning point in my life and the future of the generic drug industry. The successful outcome in that case led to my role as the architect of the legal framework for the modern generic drug industry. The Hatch-Waxman Act of 1984 laid the groundwork for the explosive growth of the US generic drug industry. Before it was enacted, generic drugs accounted for less than 20 percent of all prescriptions filled in the United States, and total sales of generic drugs were less than $1 billion. Today, 90 percent of all prescriptions are filled generically, and annual sales of generic drugs exceed $100 billion. I played an important role in that evolution as a lawyer, entrepreneur, philanthropist, advocate, and commentator.

The generic drug industry was the perfect client for me. In the 1970s, most generic drug manufacturers were small businesses owned by Jewish families. They were outsiders and underdogs trying to compete with large pharmaceutical manufacturers, America's most profitable and powerful industry. I started life as an outsider, having been born less than a year after my parents arrived in the United States as Jewish refugees from Germany two weeks before *Kristallnacht* in 1938. By the time I was in my early thirties, I had acquired the knowledge and skills to beat the insiders at their own game. As a teenager, I learned the street smarts essential to being a good lawyer, working long hours at various jobs on the Boardwalk in Atlantic City, New

Jersey, where I grew up. I experienced life in corporate America as an engineering and research assistant as part of a work/study program leading to a degree in chemical engineering.

While pursuing a law degree at night, I learned the fundamentals of the patent system as a patent examiner in the US Patent Office and as a patent agent for Esso, developed basic litigation skills as a US Department of Justice patent trial attorney, and became a seasoned litigator in private practice with a boutique New York City intellectual property law firm. I was fearless and confident and relished the David vs. Goliath opportunity to represent the interests of small generic drug manufacturers against the powerful brand name drug industry.

Generic drug manufacturers were hanging by a thread in the 1970s. They were barely profitable and did not have the capital to compete effectively. They were mostly selling very old drugs because the cost of complying with the US Food and Drug Administration's complex requirements for getting approval to sell newer ones was unaffordable. Close to one hundred important drugs on which patent protection had expired had no competition because generic manufacturers couldn't pay the cost of the required clinical trial. The industry desperately needed a change to the FDA laws governing the approval of generic drugs.

The big pharmaceutical manufacturers wanted to preserve the status quo. Perpetual monopolies allowed them to charge high prices and earn extraordinary profits. Then, as today, policymakers were concerned that the high cost of brand name medicines would make life-saving drugs unaffordable. They convinced themselves that increased competition from generic drugs was the answer. There were major stumbling blocks. Most doctors didn't know the generic name of the drugs they were prescribing. They used the brand name to write prescriptions. That changed in 1972 when Kentucky enacted a law that allowed a pharmacist to substitute a lower-cost generic drug made by a different manufacturer on a prescription written for a branded drug. By 1979, the Federal Trade Commission had concluded that automatic substitution of generic drugs by pharmacists was essential to protect consumers and urged every state to enact a law allowing it.

To blunt the adverse impact of this new competition, the pharmaceutical lobby stepped up its campaign to create concern about the quality and equivalence of generic drugs and began suing generic manufacturers to stop them from copying the size, color, or shape of the branded drug; they also sought new federal legislation to extend the life of pharmaceutical patents for up to seven years, claiming that longer patent life was justified because of the time lost while the FDA decided if a new drug was sufficiently safe and effective to warrant approval for sale.

The Generic Pharmaceutical Industry Association (GPIA) was formed in 1980 to combat these threats and develop a strategy for obtaining changes to the law that would expedite the FDA's approval of generic drugs. GPIA retained me as their patent lawyer. I conceived and negotiated the critical patent provisions of the Drug Price Competition and Patent Term Restoration Act of 1984, better known as the Hatch-Waxman Act. That law has endured until now and, together with its counterpart for biological medicines, the Biologics Price Competition and Innovation Act of 2010 (BPCIA) governs competition between brand and generic drugs.

One of the most controversial provisions of Hatch-Waxman automatically prohibited the FDA from approving a generic drug for thirty months whenever the owner of the brand name drug claimed that the generic copy would infringe a patent covering the original drug. It was a compromise designed to protect pharmaceutical companies from damages for willful patent infringement by small generic manufacturers that didn't have the money to pay damages if they were held liable for patent infringement. But, in exchange, I created the opportunity for generic manufacturers to prove that the patent blocking their approval should never have been granted before they began commercial sales. That eliminated the possibility of financial liability, even if they were wrong. The reward for a successful patent challenge was a six-month head start in the market before other generics could be approved.

The potential financial reward was enormous. A pill that a branded manufacturer sold for a dollar when a monopoly existed costs only one or two cents to manufacture. A generic version would usually sell for three or four cents in a competitive generic market where the product was available from several sources. But if only one generic is available due to a successful patent challenge, it could sell for sixty cents and capture the lion's share of the market in weeks because state laws require the automatic substitution of a lower-cost generic on prescriptions written for the brand name product.

Generic manufacturers lacked the expertise to determine which patents might be invalid and could not afford to hire lawyers to litigate complex patent issues. My years of experience, going back to my days as a patent examiner, convinced me that many pharmaceutical patents were being granted because pharmaceutical companies failed to tell the Patent Office the whole truth regarding the differences between what was known and what was claimed to be an invention worthy of a patent. I created a venture with Schein Pharmaceutical/Danbury Pharmacal to challenge the validity of patents that should never have been granted and to launch generic versions of those drugs. Schein developed and sought FDA approval for generic drugs I identified as having weak patents. I litigated the patents. We agreed to share the profits if a patent was declared invalid and we could enter the market early. Over ten years, working alone, without even a secretary, I successfully challenged the patents on seven important drugs. We made a fortune. Our success led to the creation of a patent challenge industry that files hundreds of new challenges annually and has filed over 10 thousand challenges since Hatch-Waxman became law.

Burned out from the stress of working alone and anxious to start a new life after losing my first wife to cancer, I stopped practicing law in 1995 at the age of fifty-six. But I decided to continue advocating for affordable healthcare and prescription drugs as a philanthropic endeavor. I founded the Engelberg Center on Innovation Law & Policy at NYU Law School to bring a scholarly perspective to the creation of the law governing intellectual property; created and funded Consumer Reports Best Buy Drugs to advance the use of comparative clinical effectiveness and cost information in selecting the best medication to treat a patient; instigated the Cipro controversy during the Anthrax scare to call attention to the government's right to buy drugs without regard to patents; and created the Engelberg Center for Healthcare Reform at the Brookings Institution to focus on bending the curve in healthcare costs. When it became clear that Hatch-Waxman and other laws were not lowering the overall cost of drugs or stimulating greater innovation, I became an advocate for changing the law. I wrote many articles describing how large pharmaceutical companies manipulated the patent system to delay generic competition and maintain high drug prices, used my political contacts to lobby for changes to the law and became a mentor to the next generation of scholars and advocates on these issues.

History provides the best roadmap for the future. The decades I spent helping to define how competition between brand and generic drugs would be managed and the impact of government policy on that competition gave me a unique perspective on why the United States pays the highest prices in the world for prescription drugs. Hatch-Waxman succeeded beyond everyone's wildest expectations by creating a market in which 90 percent of all prescriptions are filled with a generic drug. But the paltry 10 percent market share for patented, brand name prescriptions accounts for 82.5 percent of prescription drug expenditures. Inflation-adjusted per capita spending on prescription drugs has increased more than sevenfold in the last forty years despite the explosive growth in the use of generic medicines. It is almost double the average per capita spending in European countries. Simply put, brand name drug manufacturers have inflated the price of new drugs to compensate for their loss of profits from older drugs on which patents have expired.

Robust generic competition is essential to assuring affordable prices for older medicines. But how much patients spend on drugs is determined by how long the monopoly over a medicine lasts and the prices charged while the monopoly exists. Brand name manufacturers now focus on "product life cycle management" rather than inventing new drugs. They game FDA regulations, the Hatch-Waxman Act, the BPCIA, and the patent laws by making meaningless changes to an approved drug to build patent thickets to delay generic competition while aggressively imposing annual price increases. A system intended to spur greater innovation has failed because it is easier to earn excessive profits by prolonging the monopoly on an old drug than by inventing a new one.

Ultimately, Hatch-Waxman made older medicines far less expensive and new drugs far more costly than before the law existed. Unfortunately, some of the savings that patients should have enjoyed from the increased use of generic drugs went into the pockets of insurers, pharmacy benefit managers, and pharmacies because the government failed to regulate the distribution channels for generic drugs and to demand transparency about the enormous price difference between brand and generic drugs. Middlemen used their monopoly power to cut generic manufacturing profits to unsustainably low levels while taking an excessive slice of the difference between the generic and brand price as profits. That led to critical shortages for some older drugs and high prices for others as generic manufacturers went bankrupt or merged.

Hatch-Waxman is also becoming irrelevant. Almost half of drug spending is now on biologic drugs covered by the BPCIA. That law does not even pretend to create the balance Hatch-Waxman sought. It assures that most new biologics have no competition for a generation due to patent thickets. True generic competition does not even exist after that since most biologic drugs are approved as "biosimilar," meaning they cannot be automatically substituted on a prescription written for the brand name medicine under state laws. The price of biologic drugs often exceeds $50,000 per patient. Discounts for biosimilars are significantly smaller than the 90 percent discount for small molecule drugs covered by Hatch-Waxman. Even the co-pays for biosimilars can be unaffordable for many patients.

The PhRMA lobby claims that the high cost of drugs results from the cost of research to discover them. It simply isn't true. The federal government spends over $50 billion annually to support basic biomedical research at the nation's leading academic medical centers and universities. Outdated laws allow academia to own the patents resulting from federally funded research and sell them to pharmaceutical companies with no restraint on prices despite the government's contribution to the discovery of the drug. Biotech startups depend on technology platforms and patent portfolios financed by government research grants. Large pharmaceutical companies no longer invest in basic research but acquire the fruits of federally funded research and turn them into expensive new drugs. We have socialized the cost and risk of discovering new drugs and privatized the profits. Taxpayers pay twice. Once for the discovery of a medicine and a second time to enrich the pharmaceutical industry.

There is no greater spur to innovation than the looming expiration of a patent. The drug price crisis will continue until policymakers learn from the mistakes of the last forty years and overhaul our prescription drug and patent systems so that extraordinary profits can only be earned by innovating rather than price gouging. That is not likely to occur so long as elected officials remain dependent on contributions from pharmaceutical companies to win elections.

Chapter One

MY FIRST GENERIC DRUG CLIENT

IT WAS THE EARLY 1970s. I was in my early thirties and practicing law as a young partner at Amster & Rothstein, a small intellectual property boutique in New York City. My career was off to a flying start. I had recently won a trade secrets trial in a New York state court and a patent infringement case in the Miami federal court. I had no clients of my own. My only experience with pharmaceutical patents was a brief involvement in defending the United States as a Justice Department trial lawyer in the late 1960s for importing a low-cost generic version of a patented tranquilizer drug for use by the military. So, I was surprised and momentarily flattered when I received a call from a bank in New Jersey asking if I would be interested in representing Premo Pharmaceutical in a patent infringement litigation filed by Upjohn in the federal court in New York. Premo was charged with infringing a patent on Orinase (tolbutamide), the first oral anti-diabetic drug.

"Why are you calling me?" I asked, hoping the answer would relate to my recent victories. Instead, the bank representative told me Premo was bankrupt, and its regular patent lawyer had refused to take the case.

"We only have $10,000 to spend on this matter," the banker told me. I knew a trial would cost at least $250,000. The offer was an insult.

I should have hung up immediately. Instead, I asked if Premo had any evidence to support a claim that the tolbutamide patent was invalid. I was told that tolbutamide was a member of a class of sulfa drugs studied in dogs during World War II as a possible wound treatment. One of the side effects discovered in those studies was that the drug lowered the dogs' blood sugar. Premo claimed this prior knowledge was sufficient to make it obvious that tolbutamide can be used to lower blood sugar in people who have diabetes.

It sounded far-fetched to me. My experience with the law governing the patentability of chemical compounds made me skeptical that this evidence was enough to convince a court that the first commercially important drug for treating diabetes orally rather than by injection was not patentable. Nevertheless, I decided to accept Premo as a client with the proviso I could withdraw when the $10,000 ran out at my customary charge of sixty dollars per hour. It was a completely audacious decision that no other lawyer I knew would have made. But a plan for a quick settlement on favorable terms had already formed in my mind.

The litigation was pending before Judge Milton Pollack in the Southern District of New York. The New York courts did not like patents very much. They believed in free markets and thought patents were a limited exception to the antitrust laws reserved for only the most meritorious discoveries. More than half of the patent cases in New York resulted in a decision that the patent should not have been granted.

I had previously appeared before Judge Pollack and was confident I could take advantage of what I had learned about him. Judge Pollack had an anti-patent reputation. He also liked to push cases to trial quickly and was impatient with lawyers who tried to delay trials by getting bogged down in procedural motions or pretrial discovery. As an experienced litigator, he understood that cases tend to get settled on the eve of a trial when lawyers and clients focus more on the cost and risk of going forward.

Within weeks after I accepted the case, Judge Pollack scheduled a preliminary conference. With much bravado, I told the judge it was a simple case involving a patent that should not have been granted. We would not need much discovery and wanted an early trial date. Judge Pollack was happy to oblige. Upjohn was trapped. It had nothing to gain from a trial. It would cost Upjohn hundreds of thousands of dollars, and there would be no chance of recovering any money from an already bankrupt defendant if it won. Upjohn would lose millions in profits to new generic competitors if it lost and the patent was declared invalid. It was a "no-win" situation for Upjohn.

Upjohn didn't take long to realize that paying Premo for a certain outcome made more sense than paying its lawyers for an uncertain result. The fact that I was an experienced patent litigator with prior success in invalidating patents didn't hurt. We reached a deal quickly. Upjohn paid Premo $400,000 to sign a consent judgment acknowledging that the Upjohn patent was valid and infringed. Premo was able to pay off its creditors and continue in business. My fee didn't come close to the $10,000 limit.

Premo and most other generic drug companies were small private businesses run by Jewish families. The news that a young Jewish patent lawyer had rescued Premo from bankruptcy spread like wildfire. Who was Al Engelberg, and how did he manage to outsmart Upjohn?

Chapter Two

THE ROAD TO BECOMING A PATENT LAWYER

I WAS BORN IN DERBY, Connecticut on August 26, 1939, just ten months after my parents arrived on the *St. Louis* as Jewish refugees from Nazi Germany. But I always say that I am from Atlantic City, New Jersey, because my memories of Derby are sparse.

My father, Leo, had been a traveling salesman in Germany during the hyperinflation of the 1920s. He spoke seven languages fluently, was a brilliant chess player, and was among the smartest people I have ever known. Yet he worked as a janitor and night watchman at the Atlantic City Electric Company for his entire life. Leo drank a lot and had a violent temper, which often led to verbal and physical abuse of the family. After his death at age sixty, I learned that many of his siblings had bipolar disorder, and it seems likely that he was also afflicted.

The best thing my father ever did for me was to teach me how to play chess. I won a few medals in junior high school but have not played since. I still remember Leo emphasizing the importance of recognizing the consequences of your move and trying to figure out the moves your opponent would make. The farther ahead you could see, the more likely you could control the game. Chess became a conscious metaphor for how I eventually practiced law and was important to my success. I wasn't necessarily smarter than my adversaries. But I spent more time anticipating their arguments and was never surprised.

My mother, Gusti, was born in Munich in 1910 and well-educated. She had not worked in Germany but had learned to sew. She opened a cleaning and tailoring shop in Atlantic City, and we lived in five rooms behind the store. My parents separated when I was about nine years old. There were no lawyers involved and no child support. My mother hammered home a simple message from the earliest days of my childhood: if you want things, you must earn them. If you want a successful life, you must work hard and get a good education. It's all up to you. The message wasn't delivered in a mean-spirited way or to deny us the necessities of life. I never felt poor growing up. But my most vivid childhood memories are of how I earned money.

I began earning money when I was eight or nine years old by searching for coins under the Atlantic City Boardwalk below hot dog stands and arcades where people were likely to drop change and collecting deposits on bottles left on the beach. A little later, I began taking my wagon to the local supermarket on Saturday and offering to carry groceries home for older women. I still remember lingering by the checkout counter and calling out, "Take your order for a quarter."

I was twelve when I got my first summer job working at the candy store and soda fountain for Jack Goldberg. Jack was a kind man who taught me how to keep track of inventory and work as a soda jerk, making sodas, milkshakes, and sundaes. A soda was a nickel, but a glass of seltzer was only two cents. Many of our customers came from a nearby kosher hotel and would ask, with a Yiddish accent, for "two cents plain with a dash of cherry."

Jack taught me to say, "Oh. You want cherry soda. That's a nickel." It's funny now, but learning to interact with customers when you are only twelve was a big deal.

Over the next few summers, I went from one traditional job to the next: a beach chair concession where you worked solely for tips; Hi-Hat Joe's, a famous Boardwalk hot dog stand notorious for underpaying the staff because the owner expected you to steal part of your income by making change out of an open cash register without ringing up the sale; and Junior's, a more reputable hot dog stand where you worked hard but could make twenty-five dollars/week without stealing. At fifteen, I graduated to a job at a Boardwalk bingo parlor called "Thrillo," which was run by local mobsters. It was a gambling game that skirted the law by pretending to give away stuffed animals because cash prizes were illegal. Each customer could play as many bingo cards as they wished. There were green cards at three for a dime and gold cards that cost a dime but had bigger payoffs. The game took place in a room with six aisles with about twenty-five seats in each aisle. My job was to collect the money from one aisle. I made change from an apron full of dimes by squeezing out the correct number of dimes between my thumb and forefinger. In no time, you learned to apply just the right amount of pressure to make the right change automatically so you could complete the collection process for an entire aisle in two or three minutes.

The house tried to track how much money you had collected by sending a college kid down the aisle behind you to count how many dimes you should have collected. There was no way to get an accurate count because many players cheated by taking extra cards from the rack after they paid. But the counters deliberately undercounted. Every ninety minutes, after about twenty-five games, you would get a fifteen-minute break so the accountant in the back room could reconcile the money in your apron. Just before your break, depending on how busy it was, the counter would tell you to remove a dollar or two from your apron before turning it in. That money was shared with the counter.

I earned a $60/week salary for a five-day week from noon until 2 a.m., with a couple of hours off for dinner and frequent 15-minute breaks. The miscount added another $40/week. I was making more money than my father.

When people ask me where I learned to practice law, I always say, "Everything important I learned in Atlantic City by the time I was sixteen." The rest were just legal rules. The Boardwalk was a demanding environment in which small business owners were trying to make enough money in the ten weeks of the summer season to survive all year. Kids were trying to make money for college. Everyone cut corners. Everyone was stealing. It was a life lesson in human behavior that served me well in practicing law. The behavior doesn't change much, whether in a board room or on a boardwalk.

I was blessed with a great memory and excelled in school without any effort. I rarely took notes in class, a habit that continued through college, law school, and my legal career. I learned by listening and reading. Science and math were my favorite subjects and came easily to me. At age fifteen, I decided to study engineering in college, although I knew nothing about the field. It was a practical decision. I had to graduate from college with an education that would provide secure employment; liberal arts, medical, or law school were financially out of the question. I chose Drexel Institute of Technology in Philadelphia because it offered a five-year work/study program. After the first year, you spent six months in school and six months in a paid engineering job. The pay was enough to cover living expenses for the full year.

I saved enough money from summer jobs to pay for my first year of living expenses, but I still needed to find $700 each year for tuition and books. My mother could not afford it. Drexel provided a half-tuition scholarship for my first year. The Avoda Club of Atlantic City awarded me a $2,000 scholarship. Avoda was a Jewish version of the Rotary Club. Its members were the leading Jewish doctors, lawyers, accountants, and businesspeople of Atlantic City. They gave the annual scholarship award to a Jewish boy with a strong record of academic accomplishment, leadership, and financial need. Winning was a big honor. It also provided enough money to cover most of my tuition at Drexel for the first four years. It was an early life lesson in the importance of philanthropy that I never forgot.

"Down between two old warehouses stands an awful wreck. God created hell on earth and called it Drexel Tech." That is the song we sang at fraternity beer parties to the tune of "Far Above Cayuga's Waters" even though it was Cornell University's alma mater. It captured how I felt about Drexel for five long years. The Drexel campus was a few buildings that stretched from 32nd and Chestnut Streets toward the railroad tracks and Penn Station at 30th and Market Streets. Warehouses and a printing plant for *The Philadelphia Bulletin* surrounded it. That was it! It was a ten-minute walk through a run-down and mostly poor Black neighborhood to Drexel's student housing. Ninety-five percent of the student body lived at home and commuted. The rest of us lived in one of ten fraternity houses. They had been elegant mansions in the early twentieth century, but most had become dilapidated firetraps.

Academically, the first two years of engineering school were mostly a waste of time. Basic math and science didn't go much beyond what I had learned in high school, except for courses on using a slide rule and mechanical drawing. The last three years were a nightmare with six or seven engineering courses crammed into a ten-week quarter that required thirty-five hours per week of class and lab time, more homework than was humanly possible to complete, and constant exams. At the end of the ten weeks, there were two weeks of final exams. The continuous stress forced us to survive on five hours of sleep. Except for a few courses like organic chemistry and liberal arts courses like logic and philosophy, I was totally disinterested. There was no time to learn anything. I memorized most of the many equations designed to solve problems in basic physics, electrical, mechanical, and chemical engineering without understanding or caring much about what problems they could solve in the real world. I did well on exams simply by figuring out which equations could be solved with the data in the exam question. I felt like an idiot savant, often feeling lost and sometimes suffering from anxiety attacks. But I had a relentless drive to succeed and somehow made Dean's list and was inducted into Tau Beta Pi, the national engineering honor society.

The work program at Drexel changed my life. I thought it would just be a way to pay for my education. Its real value was the opportunity to see the future. I loved the experience of working in the real world alongside individuals who were pursuing their careers. It was an important part of my transition from being a child to becoming an adult. It was also like being Scrooge in *A Christmas Carol* and having the opportunity to see what the future had in store for me—and what I saw did not appeal to me. I realized I could never be happy working as an engineer or for a big corporation.

In July 1957, I began my first six-month job at Alan Wood Steel in Conshohocken, Pennsylvania as a lab technician working in the open-hearth chemistry lab of the steel mill. My job was to collect samples of molten steel from the open hearth and analyze them to ensure the steel contained the right percentages of manganese, chromium, and other elements that give steel sheets the properties required to make refrigerators, cars, and other products. I was on shift work and rotated between the day shift (8 a.m. to 4 p.m.), the swing shift (4 p.m. to midnight), and the graveyard shift (midnight until 8 a.m.). While it was the work of a blue-collar technician and did not require a college education, it was an eye-opening experience for a seventeen-year-old to work alongside union members in a hot and grimy environment and get first-hand exposure to basic manufacturing. It was far from the carnival atmosphere of the Boardwalk. Occasionally, I would grab a shot and a beer at 8 a.m. at the end of the graveyard shift and learn about the lives of the union laborers who were my co-workers.

My second work experience, six months later, was as an engineering assistant at DuPont's Seaford, Delaware nylon plant. In the 1950s, DuPont was one of the great chemical companies in America and employed the best and brightest engineers in the country. The manufacture of nylon yarn was a complicated process. It started on an upper floor of the factory where small nylon pellets were melted in a vat. The molten nylon flowed by gravity through a spinneret, a device that looked like a showerhead, to form the nylon into individual filaments. The filaments passed through a series of cooling, stretching, heating, and lubricating steps, allowing them to reach a certain thickness and strength. Eventually, the filaments were twisted together to form yarn, rolled up on spools, and packed for shipment. I worked with a group of engineers responsible for maintaining and improving the yield from certain product lines. We patrolled the entire manufacturing process, spotting problem areas that reduced production efficiency and responding to breakdowns in the manufacturing process. It was highly responsible work in which the engineers constantly reacted to problems and found innovative solutions.

Many of the engineers were recent college graduates. They became friends and mentors. I was invited to their homes and met their wives and babies. What I learned convinced me that I could never live the life of an engineer. Company policy prohibited vertical promotions allowing employees to become their former peers' supervisors. Almost every promotion resulted in a move to one of several DuPont nylon plants in the mid-Atlantic states. The company would guarantee the profitable sale of your home, help you buy a new one, and cover all the moving expenses. But being forced to uproot your family every few years made no sense to me and was very difficult for families.

DuPont was interested in grooming me for permanent employment after graduation and invited me back to Seaford for a second six-month work period with a significant pay raise and increased responsibility. I turned it down and accepted a research assistant position at another DuPont division in Gibbstown, New Jersey. There, I worked with a group of PhD chemists searching for a new catalyst to improve the yield of the chemical that was the primary ingredient in producing Orlon, another synthetic fiber popular in garment fabrics in the 1950s. My job was to operate a bench-scale reactor in a chemistry lab. Working under the direction of Ph. D. chemists, we prepared and tested hundreds of compounds at various concentrations, temperatures, and pressures, hoping to find a combination that would have greater efficiency than the existing commercial catalyst. The work was typical of industrial research to find new products or improve old ones.

After several months, the chemists asked me to develop a better system to keep track of all our experiments so we could more easily determine which modifications produced the best results and the most promising directions for future research. It was quite a challenge. Computer systems for this type of analysis did not yet exist. I found a manual system for data tracking and modified it to be useful for analyzing the data from the hundreds of catalysts we had tested. Gibbstown was a great learning and growth experience. It was invaluable to my subsequent career as a patent lawyer because of what I learned about how inventions are made in industrial settings. But the experience reinforced my certainty that I was not cut out for life as a scientist in a large corporation.

By the time I reached my last year at Drexel, I had decided to follow the path of a few older fraternity brothers and attend night law school while working as a patent examiner in the U.S. Patent Office. So I rejected the idea of spending another six months working for DuPont. Instead, I accepted a National Science Foundation grant to do an independent research project in Drexel's chemical engineering department and a position as a laboratory instructor for a freshman chemistry class at Drexel.

In June 1961, I graduated from Drexel and began a six-week training class to learn the basics of patent examining. Out of one thousand patent examiners, over 60 percent were recent engineering school graduates attending night law school at George Washington, Georgetown, or American University. The annual turnover in the Patent Office was 20 percent because the young examiners left for better jobs as soon as they completed law school. The small percentage of career patent examiners were mostly older men who started working in the Patent Office during the Great Depression and returned after serving in World War II. The younger examiners were like me: they came from working-class families, had chosen engineering school for financial reasons, disliked it, and decided to pursue a career in patent law.

Examining a patent application to determine if it is worthy of a patent differed greatly from my prior work experiences. To be patentable, an invention had to be "novel," which meant it could not be identical to something described in an earlier patent or publication. Patent examiners made that determination by reviewing stacks of prior patents stored in miles of file cabinets arranged by subject matter. The patent application was rejected if you found an earlier patent that described the identical idea. Usually, there were some differences between what was disclosed earlier and what was being claimed as an invention. An examiner had to decide whether those differences "would have been obvious to a person of ordinary skill in the field." It was a highly subjective judgment that required the examiner to either know something about the skills of those working in the field or try to figure it out from reading other patents and publications related to the subject matter. Most examiners had never worked in the fields they were examining and were clueless about the level of ordinary skill in that field or what might or might not be obvious. Many were recent college graduates with no industrial experience of any kind.

Fortunately, I was assigned to examine patent applications for producing synthetic fibers like nylon. My experience working in DuPont's nylon plant gave me a significant advantage. Many patent applications claimed ideas involving the routine common sense we used every day to fix production problems. Because of my familiarity with the subject matter, I could learn and apply the rules of patent examination faster and with greater confidence than most of my peers. Within a few months, I was promoted to writing briefs in cases where a patent examiner's final rejection of a patent application was being appealed to a higher tribunal within the Patent Office.

It didn't take me long to realize that the quality of the patents being granted by the US government was not very good and that many of the disputes over whether a patent was valid or infringed would never arise if patent examiners had the skills and tools they needed to make the highly subjective decision to grant a patent. In addition to lacking experience in the fields they were assigned, examiners didn't have the time or library resources to do the job properly. Examiners primarily searched through prior patents and had limited access to textbooks and journal articles that often contained better information about the general knowledge in a field. Examiners also had quotas on the number of applications they needed to review each quarter, which limited the time to study each application thoroughly. Often, we spent some of that time studying for our law school classes while pretending to search for previous patents. Law school notes were routinely cut down to fit into the uniquely sized file drawers that held the prior patents. That made it easy to create the appearance that you were studying a prior patent when you were reading your notes on contracts or torts. It was like my experience on the Boardwalk, except we were stealing time instead of money.

When big companies are sued for patent infringement, they spend months and large sums of money searching worldwide for prior patents and publications to prove that there is nothing new in a patent. They often get a court to declare a patent invalid based on previous publications and patents far more relevant than the patent examiner found. That remains true even though patent examiners use computers to conduct their searches.

For all the flaws in the system, the time I spent as a patent examiner was priceless. The content of a patent application and its examination history is the most important document in patent litigations. Personal experience with how that history is created gives you a unique insight you cannot get from reading the file. The patent laws state that every issued patent is presumed valid, and a party challenging a patent must prove invalidity by clear and convincing evidence. It is a law that defies common sense. In less than a year as an examiner, I learned that the patent system was a mess and granted too many bad patents. That knowledge had a profound influence on my career.

About eight months after I began working in the Patent Office, a white-haired gentleman named Henry "Turk" Sherman walked into my cubicle and said: "Come outside. I want to talk to you." Everyone knew Turk. He was the senior partner of a Washington patent law firm that handled day-to-day issues with patent applications for several Fortune 500 companies.

Once outside, Turk pitched me on the idea of leaving the Patent Office to accept a position as a patent agent at Esso Research in Elizabeth, New Jersey. He told me that spending three more years as a patent examiner was a waste of time. I could learn far more by working with inventors and writing patent applications. I would also get a big raise in salary plus $1,000 a year to cover law school tuition. Just one year after becoming a patent examiner, I became a registered patent agent for Esso Research. I was a second-year night school student at NYU Law School living in a fourth-floor Greenwich Village walk-up.

After five years of engineering school, law school was a breath of fresh air. Legal reasoning involves many of the same analytical processes used to solve an equation, except you are working with words and ideas, not numbers. Initially, I lacked the experience in writing that is essential to excel in law school. That changed due to one lecture that profoundly affected not only my writing but also how I practiced law and trained young lawyers. A professor emphasized that the answer to a legal question must express the reasons for your conclusions and not just conclusions. Often, there is no right answer. In the real world, the lawyer who presents the most compelling reasons for how and why a legal matter should be resolved is the winner.

The Esso patent department employed fifty professionals. Eight of us were attending law school at night. I was assigned to work with a group responsible for ensuring that the research output of a group of petrochemical scientists was patented. Those flaming stacks you see when driving by a refinery are distillation columns that divide a barrel of oil into different chemicals based on their boiling points. The chemicals are eventually converted into higher-value products like lubricants, pesticides, plastics, and hundreds of other products. The oil companies develop and patent these products to get more profit from a barrel of oil.

I worked with a group of petrochemical scientists to ensure they kept written records of their research experiments and encouraged them to submit their best ideas for patent protection. We met regularly to review those submissions, determine if they met the legal standards for a patent, drafted the patent applications, and steered them through the process of obtaining a patent. My knowledge of chemistry, research experience at DuPont, and my stint as a patent examiner gave me the experience to do my job well with minimal supervision.

Turk Sherman was right. I was getting far more valuable experience at Esso than I would have by remaining in the Patent Office. Work and law school reinforced each other. I was learning legal reasoning in the evening and applying what I learned in my day job. But I didn't particularly like working for a big corporation. I wanted to control my destiny and thought about becoming a trial lawyer and joining a law firm. We would take a coffee break every afternoon, and a group of law students and career lawyers would gossip for twenty minutes. Many of our discussions centered on career opportunities, especially at New York City patent law firms.

In those days, no major law firm in the country had a patent practice. Small, specialized law firms practiced patent, trademark, and copyright law. The largest patent firms had fewer than fifty lawyers. The older lawyers knew the firms well and would critique them. "Most of them have no Jewish lawyers," they'd say. "There are a couple of small Jewish firms, but they don't have Fortune 500 clients."

Another popular theme was that the firms were very conservative and did not give young associates real training or opportunities to become litigators. "They are not going to let you try a case. You will carry a partner's bag for ten years;" "You will be thirty-five or forty before you get to take a deposition, and it will only happen when a partner gets sick." These arguments against joining a law firm were repeated over and over and served to discourage me from looking for a job in private practice after graduating from law school.

Charlie Barris, one of the older Esso lawyers, mentioned that he had a friend working as a patent trial attorney at the US Department of Justice. That sounded interesting, so I followed up. The patent section of the Civil Division defended the US government against claims for patent infringement. It sounded perfect, except that the starting salary for law school graduates was $5,000 less than my current salary and $10,000 less than the starting salary Esso had offered me as a graduate lawyer. I didn't care. I graduated from law school, took the New York bar exam, and returned to Washington, DC to become a trial lawyer.

On my first day at the Justice Department, T. Hayward Brown, the chief of the Patent Section, came into my office carrying a stack of files. Hayward was a good ol' boy from Alabama in his late sixties. He had been with the government since the Depression. We chatted for a while, and then I asked about the files. "What are those?"

He responded in his Southern drawl, "Son, those are your cases."

I said, "What do I do with them?"

He smiled and said, "I only have two pieces of advice for you. The first olive is the toughest one to get out of the jar. And if you get too far out of line, the judge or your opponent will straighten you out."

That was it! I assumed there would be a formal training program, but it would be sink or swim. It was a scary moment. Was I going to learn to be a trial lawyer on my own?

Fortunately, the patent section was a collegial place. Hayward's door was always open for advice and a few stories to go with it.

The US government is immune from claims of patent infringement. Neither the government nor its suppliers can be sued in the federal courts to prevent infringement or collect damages. A special law, 28 USC §1498, allows a patent owner to sue the government in the United States Court of Claims to recover reasonable compensation if a valid patent has been infringed. It is like an eminent domain proceeding where the government takes part of your land to build a highway: you can't prevent it, but you are entitled to compensation. The government has the same defenses to a claim for compensation that a private defendant would have for patent infringement. It can claim that the patent was not infringed or invalid and should not have been granted.

The primary job of the Patent Section was to represent the government in cases seeking compensation for patent infringement. About seventy-five to one hundred infringement cases were pending in the Patent Section. A law firm with that many active litigations would employ at least one hundred lawyers, and they would be working around the clock. We only had seventeen lawyers, who mostly worked from nine to five except when they were on trial. There were a couple of reasons why the environment was so laid back. First, you don't have a client when the government is your client. The Treasury pays compensation for successful claims, and the payment has no impact on the budget of any federal agency. There was nobody who cared if you won or lost a case. Also, for most large government procurements, the government had no liability. Its suppliers were required to reimburse the government for any compensation the government was ordered to pay.

The potential liability of a government supplier could amount to millions of dollars. They were very knowledgeable about the flaws in a patent and retained the best patent lawyers in the country to assist the government's lawyer in defending against claims. But, only the Justice Department lawyers could represent the government in the US Court of Claims. All any law firm partner could do was sit next to you and give you advice and assistance in preparing the case for trial. It was ironic. I had decided to delay going into private practice because I did not want to carry a partner's bag. As a Justice Department lawyer, those partners were, in effect, carrying my bag.

In one of my cases involving nuclear fuel pellets, the government's supplier had a potential liability of tens of millions. The supplier retained Ed Luedeka and Julius Tabin of Anderson, Luedeka, Fitch, Even & Tabin, a highly regarded Chicago patent firm, to assist me. I worked with Ed and Julius for over a year, preparing the case for trial. We spent a week in California taking critical depositions. Ed sat beside me, passing notes or whispering in my ear to correct my mistakes or make suggestions as I conducted the examinations. During the breaks and at dinner every night, he would critique my performance and help me strategize about the line of questioning for the following day. The experience was priceless. I was only twenty-six years old and was lead counsel, getting assistance and advice from lawyers with decades of experience.

Commissioners of the Court of Claims conduct patent trials. They perform the same function as a federal district court judge in a patent case between private parties, except their decisions are not final. A panel of the Court of Claims reviewed every case. The review process was analogous to an appeal to a federal appellate court from a trial conducted in a federal district court. I inherited several cases that had been tried before I arrived at the Justice Department but were decided after the lawyer who conducted the trial had resigned to enter private practice. That allowed me to write briefs supporting or opposing the Commissioner's decision and present oral arguments before the Court of Claims. Few patent lawyers get to do this type of appellate work until decades after they are admitted to the bar.

I also had the rare opportunity to brief and argue an appeal before the nation's highest patent court, the Court of Customs and Patent Appeals. I represented the US Army in *In re Mod*, an appeal from the US Patent Office's decision to refuse to grant a patent on a new chemical compound discovered in an Army research laboratory. The *Mod* case raised a legal question concerning the standard for patenting a new chemical compound similar in molecular structure to a class of existing chemical compounds. Chemists often make minor molecular changes to a known class of compounds, hoping the change produces a superior or unexpected improvement in some useful property. That was the type of research I did at DuPont. The prevailing law, before *Mod*, was that it would be obvious to a skilled chemist that a compound structurally similar to a known compound would have properties and uses similar to the known compounds. Therefore, a structurally similar compound cannot be patented unless it has a new or unexpectedly superior property.

In *Mod*, the Army had discovered a new member of a class of compounds known to be useful as insecticides. It also discovered that its new compound and the known compounds were useful as antimicrobial agents. On the appeal, I argued that Mod's compound should be patentable because its antimicrobial activity was new and unexpected. The court disagreed. It held that the new compound was not patentable because its properties were no different from the existing compounds. Mod had discovered a new use for a known class of compounds rather than a new compound. Little did I know that twenty years after my involvement in *Mod*, the knowledge I gained from that case about the legal standard for patenting a chemical compound would become the foundation for my involvement in challenging pharmaceutical patents.

I also got my first exposure to generic drugs as a Justice Department lawyer. Carter-Wallace, a pharmaceutical manufacturer, sued the United States for purchasing a generic version of Miltown, a popular tranquilizer. The Defense Department had purchased large quantities of a generic version of Miltown from Scandinavian sources at a 90 percent discount from the brand name drug. These purchases were made under a ruling by the Office of the Comptroller General that government agencies should ignore patents when purchasing drugs or other products because of the government's patent immunity. Carter-Wallace claimed they were entitled to recover their lost profits as reasonable compensation, an amount that was more than ten times the government's acquisition cost for the drug. The issue was never decided because an unrelated case declared the patent invalid on technical grounds. But the case exposed me to the vast price differential between patented and generic drugs and to the ability of the government to use its patent immunity to purchase low-cost drugs.

In the fall of 1968, after more than three years at Justice, I joined the firm of Amster & Rothstein, a small Jewish patent firm in New York, bypassing offers for employment at more prestigious firms in New York and Chicago. The Amster firm had only two partners; its senior associates were law school classmates. I had far more trial experience than anyone in the firm except Mort Amster and felt I would get a greater opportunity to use it.

Mort Amster was the smartest and most aggressive lawyer I had ever met. He had an uncanny ability to immediately spot the critical issues in a case and almost as quickly foresee the best path forward. Mort was always going for the jugular. He could often be rude and dismissive to opposing lawyers, especially those he thought were second-rate. Mort's writing style matched his personality. Sentences were blunt instruments: short and punchy. Initially, he harshly criticized the more formal writing style I had been taught at Esso and in law school. I liked his style and quickly adapted to it. Being blunt can get you in trouble in polite society, but busy judges love it when you don't beat around the bush.

Nothing in my experience prepared me for the reality of the private practice of law. I was accustomed to working in large organizations where it was often difficult to understand how your work made any real difference to the enterprise. Amster & Rothstein represented mostly small and medium-sized companies that were often family-owned. The clients came to you with real problems that directly impacted their profits. Serving a client's needs was an awesome responsibility. I never lost that feeling. Clients were paying me fifty dollars/hour to produce a result. That seemed like a lot of money back then. They only spent it because they expected to profit from my advice. Accounting for the time I spent and ensuring the clients received value kept me up at night and caused a radical change in my schoolboy study habits. I never waited until the last minute to complete any project and always reviewed my work to ensure the final product was my best effort.

As I gained experience, I learned there were times when you should reduce a bill because things had not worked out well and other times when a great result justified a bigger fee. On one occasion, I turned a useless and expensive lawsuit into a merger by engaging the other side's CEO in an off-the-record conversation during a deposition. The client expressed surprise when I added $100,000 to the final bill. When I reminded him of the large monthly bills he had received while the litigation dragged on and the millions he earned from the merger, he thanked me and promptly paid the bonus. I once famously told a client, "I have hours that are worth thousands of dollars and days that aren't worth shit," and that he should fire me if he ever felt I was not producing value.

Trademarks, unfair competition, and copyright law were important to the firm's practice. We represented companies in the toy, fabric, wallpaper, and fashion industries where making copies of popular products was common. The firm had a reputation for aggressively pursuing litigation to prevent the sale of copies of our clients' products and developed techniques for getting the federal courts to block the sale of these knockoffs within a week or two from when we learned of their existence. It was quite different from the much slower pace of patent litigation and provided a unique opportunity to hone both litigation skills and deal-making skills at a very fast pace.

Preparing patent applications was also quite different in private practice than at Esso. You knew from the beginning that the patent would cover an important commercial product and would likely end up in litigation. Every word in the patent application and the arguments presented to the patent examiner had to be carefully selected to ensure that the patent would not only be granted but also withstand a court challenge. The experience made me realize another of the many flaws in the patent system. Companies spend millions on litigation to enforce patents. Yet those patents tend to be written by less experienced attorneys who don't fully appreciate that every word in the patent application and every argument made to a patent examiner in the course of getting the patent can come back to haunt you when the patent is litigated. In my private practice years, I only wrote two patent applications. One was the Aris Isotoner glove, a fashion accessory with benefits for arthritic hands, and the other was an onion ring made from chopped onions and a breading mix that Burger King popularized. Both patents produced millions of dollars for my clients, and I successfully enforced them in many patent infringement litigations.

I achieved independence quickly at the Amster firm. Early in my second year, Mort gave me primary responsibility for a trade secrets litigation, *Public Relations Aids vs. Wagner*. Wagner was a former employee of Public Relations Aids who was accused of stealing trade secrets related to the programming of an Addressograph mail labeling machine. Mort attended the trial as my second chair. By the mid-afternoon break on the first day, I turned to Mort and said: "You can't keep tugging on my sleeve, passing me notes, and whispering in my ear. It's distracting me from listening to the judge, opposing counsel, and the witnesses. I don't have time to listen to you. Go back to the office. Everything will be okay." It was an outrageous way to speak to your boss and could have ended my career. Mort left, I won the case, and the client was ecstatic. Unfortunately, the trial judge was so anxious to rule in my favor that his opinion was based on a seriously flawed legal analysis. I pleaded with the client to settle the case because I was confident we would lose if there were an appeal. My advice was rejected and the appeals court unanimously ruled against us.

The other case that stands out from that second year was a patent infringement case involving the Ray Hunt deep-V hull. To this day, it is one of the most popular fishing and racing boats of all time. Hunt had sued our client, Hurricane Boats, a small Miami boat manufacturer, for patent infringement in the Miami federal court. Our prospects were dim because the same judge had previously held the patent valid in earlier litigation against a different infringer. Any sane lawyer would have told the client that the case was unwinnable. Not Mort. He told the client we would prove the patent was invalid and should never have been granted and then turned the case over to me to make good on that promise.

There were rumors that Hunt had built several boats and used them in public more than a year before he filed his patent application. A patent is invalid unless the application is filed within a year of public use or disclosure. I spent some time in Boston, Cape Cod, and Rhode Island talking to people in the boating business who knew Hunt and might have some knowledge about when the first Hunt deep-V boat was built. My search eventually led me to a boatyard called The Anchorage in Newport, Rhode Island. They allowed me to rummage through some of their old files. I found a brochure containing a photograph of Hunt and his boat serving as a tender for Jakob Isbrandsten's entry into the America Cup sailboat races held in Newport in the summer of 1958. The brochure was not dated, but Hunt's boat had numbers on the bow that looked like a Coast Guard registration.

The Coast Guard confirmed that the Hunt boat was registered more than a year before the patent application was filed. I also learned from the Coast Guard that, years earlier, they had provided the same registration information to Hunt's attorney. I got a copy of that correspondence by filing a Freedom of Information Act request with the Coast Guard. The correspondence proved that Hunt and his attorney knew the patent was invalid and suppressed the Jacobsen tender evidence at the prior trial. If the judge had been told the truth, he would have been compelled to declare the Hunt patent invalid. Mort and I confronted Hunt's attorney with the evidence and demanded that Hunt disclaim his patent and pay our client's legal fees. He had no choice. He knew the trial judge would grant our request and refer the matter to the bar association for disciplinary action against him.

Many successful lawyers have one big case that made their reputation. Mine was *Penn Yan vs. Sea Lark Boats*. Sea Lark was a small boatyard in the Florida Keys owned by Don Wollard. Wollard had designed a new boat hull for fishing in the shallow waters of the Keys. He called it "Tunnel Drive." In a typical inboard-powered boat, the propellor and propeller shaft extend at an angle below the keel. The propeller and shaft are inside the tunnel above the keel in a tunnel drive boat. A tunnel drive boat can operate at high speed in shallow water since the propellor can't run aground. Wollard owned a patent on his tunnel drive boat.

Penn Yan, a large boat manufacturer, also had a patent on a boat hull with a tunnel and a registered trademark for "Tunnel Drive." In 1971, Penn Yan sued Sea Lark for infringement in the federal district court in Miami. Our firm's reputation had spread through the boating industry because of our victory in the Hunt case, and we were hired to represent Sea Lark.

There were several earlier patents describing boats with tunnels. The Penn Yan and Sea Lark patents were very weak, and it seemed unlikely that either would survive a court battle. However, Sea Lark's patent was earlier. That meant Penn Yan had the extra burden of proving its patent was patentable despite Sea Lark's earlier patent. That seemed impossible. I expected Penn Yan to buy or license the Sea Lark patent since they had a successful business and Sea Lark had only produced a few boats.

I was stunned when Penn Yan decided to go to trial. It was a bad decision by an arrogant partner from a prestigious Chicago patent firm, and it provided me with an opening to win a case that should have been unwinnable. Penn Yan could not vigorously attack the validity of Sea Lark's patent without sinking its own ship. That left me free to argue that the Penn Yan boat not only infringed Sea Lark's earlier patent but that Penn Yan's patent was invalid because it claimed the same invention claimed in the earlier Sea Lark patent.

The trial was before Bill Mehrtens, an experienced judge and a true Southerner. Mehrtens was a shallow-water fisherman, so he was enjoying the case. The day before the trial ended, I asked the judge if he would like to drive the boat after the trial ended so he could see for himself how it performed. He loved the idea. The boat was only twenty-five feet in length. I told Wollard to have his family and dogs on the boat before we arrived at the dock. When the judge and the lawyers arrived at the dock, we did not have enough room to board. I got the judge on board and then suggested it would be too crowded if any lawyers boarded. Opposing counsel was furious, but the judge was already on the boat and was anxious to drive the boat before darkness fell. He left without the lawyers. The next day, I asked Wollard how it went. He said, "The first question the judge asked me was how I managed to find a smart Jew lawyer from New York."

After a non-jury trial ends, each side submits a document called "Proposed Findings of Fact and Conclusions of Law." In it, you recite every important fact you have proved and explain how the law should be applied to those facts to decide the case. The trial court usually decides a case by writing its own Findings of Fact and Conclusions of Law, often by selecting or modifying the findings submitted by each party. In *Sea Lark*, Judge Mehrtens copied my entire submission. It became his decision. He just had the first page retyped to remove the word "proposed" from my findings, and the last page was retyped to remove my signature and add a place for his. It was a big victory for me and an embarrassing defeat for Penn Yan. My proposed findings ordered Penn Yan to pay our attorney's fees because Penn Yan had obtained its patent by wrongfully withholding information from the Patent Office that might have caused the patent examiner to deny it.

Penn Yan fired its Chicago lawyer and hired Bill Kerr of Fish & Neave to file an appeal to the Fifth Circuit Court of Appeals. Fish & Neave was the pre-eminent New York patent firm, and Kerr was its star litigator. Kerr opened his oral argument by stating: "My predecessor in the Court below tried to carry water on both shoulders." It was a pointed attack on the dumb strategy of the Chicago lawyer in trying to claim that the later Penn Yan patent was valid over the Sea Lark patent rather than attacking the Sea Lark patent.

Before he could get another word out of his mouth, Chief Judge John Minor Wisdom interrupted and said, "Yes, and he spilled it all over himself." Kerr then attacked Judge Mehrtens for indiscriminately copying my proposed findings. He noted that my findings contained at least eight typographical errors and claimed Judge Mehrtens shirked his responsibilities by adopting them instead of writing his own. The appeals court was unimpressed. They would not grant a new trial on a new theory or insult the trial judge's integrity when the outcome was clearly the result of bad lawyering by Penn Yan's prior attorney.

In a slap in the face to Kerr, the Fifth Circuit opinion consisted of a single sentence: "We adopt the opinion of the district court as the opinion of this Court."

I officially became a partner of Amster & Rothstein in January 1972, only three years after joining the firm. Business was booming, and the firm was growing. We moved to an elegant Park Avenue location that expressed our confidence in the future and were scrambling to hire more lawyers. At about the same time, Esso Research, my former employer, hired me to bring an action against a petrochemical competitor in Mississippi for infringement of an Esso patent. Within a year, and for legal fees of less than $25,000, we achieved a $1 million settlement. I was so proud that my former employer, one of the largest companies in the world, had expressed their confidence in me by hiring me to represent them, and I had produced a result that justified that confidence. It gave me great satisfaction to know that I had repaid them for investing in my legal education and early training and that I had made the right choice in pursuing a career in private practice.

I was thirty-two years old and on top of the world. I had found a career I loved, the independence I craved, and the opportunity to use all my skills. I was confident and eager for whatever challenge might come next.

Chapter Three

GENERIC DRUGS BEFORE 1984

MY SUCCESS REPRESENTING PREMO LED to a call from Ben Wiener, a founder of Zenith Laboratories, another small generic drug manufacturer in New Jersey. Ben invited me to meet him on a Friday afternoon at the Plaza Hotel in New York City to discuss the possibility of representing Zenith on a patent infringement matter. At the meeting, he told me that Zenith had been sued for infringement of Roche's patent on Valium. The trial was scheduled to begin in the New Jersey federal court on Monday morning. The idea of getting involved in a case three days before trial was absurd. I listened for a few minutes and said: "You don't need a lawyer; you need a rabbi to help you pray for a miracle." I declined to get involved.

By 1978, new management had taken over at Zenith following a loan default. Zenith had a negative net worth and was on the verge of bankruptcy. It hoped to revive itself by entering the market with a generic version of Eli Lilly's popular antibiotic, cephalexin. Unfortunately, Lily had sued Zenith for patent infringement and was seeking an immediate injunction to stop Zenith from making any sales. It was a far worse situation than the Premo case because the courts in New Jersey were generally biased in favor of the big pharmaceutical companies that were major employers in the state.

The basic Lilly patent on cephalexin had expired. Lilly was trying to extend its monopoly on cephalexin by claiming a more stable form of the same compound. After a brief trial, the judge held the broadest claim of the Lilly patent invalid. But he held a narrower claim valid and granted a preliminary injunction that stopped Zenith from selling its generic product. A moment of gloom suddenly turned to glee when I realized the judge had committed a major mistake. In pretrial proceedings before the judge's decision, we forced Lilly to admit that Zenith's product did not infringe the narrow claim of the patent. The judge had erroneously enjoined Zenith from selling its generic product. Instead of contacting the court, I contacted Lilly's lawyers, hoping to make a deal without asking the court to correct its mistake. Lilly agreed to purchase Zenith's generic cephalexin inventory at a premium price. The settlement gave Zenith a quick infusion of cash needed to rebuild its business.

The Lilly case solidified my reputation in the generic drug industry. Generic drug companies were the perfect client for me. Their problems allowed me to take advantage of all my life experiences, science education, and legal training. I was much more comfortable and experienced attacking patents than defending them. The role of defending the underdog against the interests of the big corporation also appealed to me. My clients were producing "knockoffs" and were not innovators. Nevertheless, they provided an essential public service by making low-cost generic medicines available.

Major obstacles stood in the way of selling generic versions of newer medicines in the 1970s. The fact that these medicines were patented was not the biggest obstacle. Getting FDA approval to market a generic drug was complicated and expensive. Before 1962, drugs were approved if they were safe. Proof of effectiveness was not required. After the law changed in 1962, you had to prove that a drug was both safe and effective, even if it was a copy of a previously approved drug. That usually required an expensive clinical trial, which most small generic manufacturers could not afford. More than one hundred new drugs approved after 1962 had no generic competition even though the patents on those drugs had expired.

If you were lucky enough to get generic approval, it wasn't easy to sell the generic product. Brand name manufacturers heavily promoted the brand name and rarely referred to a drug by its generic name. Most doctors and patients couldn't tell you the generic name of a drug. Everyone was familiar with "Valium" as the name of the leading anxiety medication, but few knew that its official name was "diazepam." If a doctor prescribed "Valium," it violated the trademark law for a pharmacist to substitute diazepam made by another manufacturer. It is the same reason a restaurant can't serve you Pepsi without your permission when you order a Coke. Coke is a trademark of the Coca-Cola Company.

Generic drug companies were mostly selling much older medicines and were barely profitable. Branded pharmaceuticals were the most profitable industry in America. They enjoyed an average annual profit of over 20 percent of sales, two to three times that of publicly traded companies. Because of their monopoly power, they could charge any price they wished. Typically, the cost of producing a medicine did not exceed 1 or 2 percent of its selling price; a pill that sold for one dollar cost a penny or two.

By the late 1970s, high prices for branded drugs led to growing public support for more generic competition. In 1978, New York state enacted the first law that allowed pharmacists to automatically substitute a generic version of a drug on a prescription written using the brand name. That meant it became legal for a pharmacist to fill a prescription for "Valium" with generic diazepam from another manufacturer. This law stripped the big drug companies of their right to sue for infringement of their trademarks. In 1979, the Federal Trade Commission (FTC) recommended that all states adopt generic substitution laws after conducting a study of the prescription drug market in which they found, "[t]he basic problem is that the forces of competition do not work well in a market where the consumer who pays does not choose, and the physician who chooses does not pay."

Brand name drug manufacturers began aggressively asserting new monopoly rights. They claimed that the size, color, and shape of a pill were entitled to protection from copying because the appearance of a tablet functioned like a trademark and identified a specific manufacturer. I defended Zenith in several cases claiming that Zenith was guilty of unfair competition because it had copied the appearance of the brand name medicine.

Patients don't choose their prescription medicines. They don't even see them until they take them home from the pharmacy and open the bottle for the first time. When they do, the pill's appearance reassures them that they got the same medicine as the last time the prescription was filled. Patient surveys proved that most patients would not take their medication if the pill looked different from the one they were accustomed to taking. They would first check with their doctor or the pharmacy to get assurances that the correct medicine had been dispensed. Many pharmacists and physicians were willing to testify about the frequent calls they got from patients when the appearance of their medication was changed. As a matter of law, proof that the appearance of a tablet served the functional purpose of identifying the medicine and not a particular source for the medicine should have been enough for the courts to dismiss the claim that copying a pill's appearance was unfair competition.

Not in New Jersey. The pharmaceutical industry was heavily concentrated there. Every elected official received bundles of cash contributions from pharmaceutical manufacturers, and every judge owed their job to some politician or worked in a law firm representing large drug manufacturers. Judges in New Jersey thought that selling generic drugs was comparable to counterfeiting. In one case where I was defending Zenith for copying the color and shape of Stelazine, a major tranquilizer, Judge Vincent Biunno suggested that Zenith's conduct was comparable to the conduct of the people who had laced Tylenol with cyanide. I was so angry that I formally accused the judge of bias against generic drugs and asked that he recuse himself from hearing our case. Generic drug manufacturers lost every case in New Jersey in which they were charged with unfair competition because they had copied the appearance of a brand name drug.

In New York, it was a different story. Judge Jack Weinstein of the Eastern District of New York ruled that the appearance of a pill was functional because it helped patients identify their medicine. Because of the conflict with the New Jersey courts, in 1981, the US Supreme Court agreed to hear *Inwood Laboratories v Ives Laboratories*, an appeal from Judge Weinstein's decision that the size, color, and shape of the drug known as Cyclospasmol was functional and not protectable as a trademark.

By 1981, eight generic drug manufacturers—Zenith, Darby, Schein, Mylan, Barr, Bolar, Par, and Biocraft—had formed a trade association known as the Generic Pharmaceutical Industry Association (GPIA). They had split off from a larger group known as the National Association of Pharmaceutical Manufacturers (NAPM), which included distributors, ingredient suppliers, and other smaller enterprises. Ken Larsen, the CEO of Zenith Laboratories, became the founding chairman of GPIA and retained me to advise the trade association on patent and trademark matters. The board of GPIA was asked for advice on who should represent the generic drug industry in the Cyclospasmol case before the Supreme Court. The choice boiled down to Milton Bass or me. Milton was a flamboyant lawyer in his late sixties who had been counsel to NAPM and the lawyer for several members of GPIA for decades. Out of respect for his age and years of service, Milton got the Supreme Court assignment but only on the condition that he would work with me to prepare the argument.

Several days before the Supreme Court was scheduled to hear the oral argument, I met with Milton to discuss his presentation. He was uncomfortable with the idea of taking any direction from a lawyer who was young enough to be his son. We chatted for a while before I said: "Milton, I want to hear the opening paragraph of your argument."

He looked at me incredulously and said, "I never prepare what I will say at an argument. I allow myself to be carried by the emotion of the moment."

I responded, "That is the dumbest fucking thing I have ever heard any lawyer say. This is the Supreme Court, and you must know your opening lines." Our conversation went downhill from there.

I cringed as Milton addressed the Supreme Court a few days later. The argument should have begun with the important role that the appearance of a pill plays in assuring patients that they are taking the right medicine, something every justice had likely experienced. Instead, Milton began with a public policy rant about the importance of low-cost generic drugs to senior citizens. It was so irrelevant and off-key that Justice Sandra Day O'Connor interrupted him to ask, "Counsel, doesn't this case involve a federal statute?" It was an embarrassing rebuke and a lost opportunity for the generic drug industry to resolve an important legal issue. GPIA had hoped the Supreme Court would agree that the appearance of a medicine could never be protected as a trademark because of its functional importance to patients in identifying their medication. Instead, the Court ruled that it was within the discretion of the trial judge, based on the specific evidence presented, to determine the answer to that question on a case-by-case basis. In practical effect, it meant that the judges in New Jersey could continue to rule against generic manufacturers based on the specific facts presented in each case. It took decades before the 3rd Circuit Court of Appeals, the court that hears appeals from the New Jersey federal district courts, eventually settled the question and held that the appearance of a medicine could not be protected because of its functional attributes.

The enactment of state generic substitution laws put pressure on the FDA to approve generic versions of drugs on which patents had expired. For decades, the FDA had been using an abbreviated process to approve generic copies of medicines approved before 1962, when the law only required proof that a drug was safe but did not require evidence of effectiveness. An Abbreviated New Drug Application (ANDA) only needed proof that the generic copy was identical to the original drug. Independent clinical trials were unnecessary.

A generic drug was the same as the branded medicine if the active ingredient was identical in chemical composition and purity and was bioequivalent when formulated into a pill. Drugs were bioequivalent if they delivered approximately the same amount of the active ingredient to the bloodstream over the same time interval. Bioequivalence could be proved by an inexpensive study in which a group of healthy individuals ingest either the brand name or generic drug and have blood samples drawn at intervals over several hours. They repeated that process a second time while taking the other version of the same drug.

If the FDA implemented the abbreviated application process for approving all generic drugs, patients would get access to low-cost versions of many popular drugs. The powerful PhRMA lobby actively opposed the abbreviated process, and it was not likely to be implemented unless Congress enacted legislation compelling its use.

Fearing that an abbreviated generic approval process might eventually be approved, brand name drug manufacturers began to lobby Congress for longer patent monopolies to delay generic competition. By 1979, federal legislation was pending that would extend the life of pharmaceutical patents by up to seven years. The Senate unanimously passed that bill in 1981. It was a potential disaster for the generic drug industry.

GPIA asked me to help present arguments against patent term extension to the House of Representatives. I was working with Bill Haddad, GPIA's CEO. Haddad had enjoyed a long career in politics and investigative journalism and was a senior official in the Peace Corps during the Kennedy administration. He had a history of antagonizing brand name pharmaceutical companies as a staffer for Senator Albert Gore Sr. (D-TN) and later for Senator Estes Kefauver (D-TN). Eventually, he worked for Governor Hugh Carey in New York, where he played an important role in enacting New York's law permitting a lower-cost generic drug to be substituted on prescriptions written for a brand name medicine. Haddad could be a loose cannon at times and would make arguments that were difficult to comprehend. But he was a likable character and a crusader for liberal causes who had a great rapport with many political leaders.

In February 1982, I testified at a hearing of the Subcommittee on Investigations and Oversight of the House Committee on Science and Technology. Al Gore, Jr., a second-term congressman from Tennessee, chaired the hearing. During that hearing, PhRMA presented studies to support its claim that the FDA approval process for approving a new drug ate up more than half of the seventeen-year life of a patent. PhRMA argued that Congress should "restore" that loss by extending the life of patents claiming new drugs by seven years.

I testified on a panel with Ken Larsen and Bill Haddad. We presented data to show that the average time before a new drug faced any generic competition was eighteen and a half years. That was ten years longer than PhRMA was claiming. PhRMA's calculations were based on the expiration date of the basic patent claiming a new drug; our data was based on when competition from a generic drug began. The expiration date of the basic patent was meaningless in defining how long a drug monopoly lasted. Pharmaceutical companies often have more than one patent preventing competition. Generic manufacturers also faced lengthy delays after a patent expired before the FDA approved the first generic version of a drug.

I also provided Congress with some basic information about patent law to counter the idea that patents guarantee inventors a market for the seventeen-year life of a patent. A patent only grants the right to exclude others from making, using, or selling a patented invention. Whether a product can be sold and for how long is determined by consumer demand, laws governing product safety, and many other factors. In some cases, like toys and games, the commercial life of a product may be less than the time it takes to get a patent. In other situations, a commercial product does not exist when the patent is granted because there is no market for the product or the patent owner lacks the capital to produce the product.

Al Gore was sympathetic to our side. But congressional hearings tend to be meaningless. Members wander in and out of the room, often talking to staff, reading documents, or napping. Teaching patent law to Congress is like training a puppy—both have short attention spans. Many are also preoccupied with political considerations that have nothing to do with the merits. Pharmaceutical companies spend lavishly on lobbying and campaign contributions, which buy the votes of many legislators. Generic manufacturers faced a monumental task in seeking to prevent patent term extension legislation from becoming law even though the arguments for granting extra patent protection for drug patents were flimsy and the industry's profits were far higher than all other industries. It was an eye-opening exposure to the world of crony capitalism.

Health Affairs was launched as a new health policy journal in 1982. The publisher invited the submission of two papers on each side of the patent term extension issue. Al Gore and I authored articles opposing patent term extension. His was entitled "Patent Term Extension: An Expensive and Unnecessary Giveaway," and mine was "Patent Term Extension: An Overreaching Solution to a Nonexistent Problem." It was a new form of advocacy for me and the first paper I had ever published.

Al Gore, Rep. Henry Waxman (D-CA), Bill Haddad, and Jim Flug were engaged in an all-out lobbying effort to convince members of the House to vote against the Senate bill. Flug was a respected Harvard-educated lawyer who had worked for Bobby Kennedy in the Justice Department and was later counsel to Sen. Ted Kennedy (D-MA) on the Senate Judiciary Committee. Haddad, with his typical journalistic flare, had taken my description of the way drug companies game the patent system by getting multiple patents on the same product and coined a word to describe it: "evergreening." That term remains popular, although "patent thickets" has more recently become a popular way to describe the phenomenon of multiple patents blocking competition long after a basic patent claiming a drug expires.

As Congress rushed toward adjournment for the mid-term elections in 1982, the House had no time to pass the patent extension bill by regular order. It was placed on the suspension calendar, which meant a two-thirds majority was required to pass the bill without debate. The legislation fell five votes short. Waxman, Gore, Haddad, and Flug had performed a miracle that paved the way for a historic compromise, even though it was likely that our side would have to give in to some form of extra patent life for pharmaceuticals.

Chapter Four

THE HATCH-WAXMAN ACT

In the new term of Congress in 1983, Henry Waxman became chair of the House Subcommittee on Health. He introduced a bill requiring the FDA to adopt the Abbreviated New Drug Application (ANDA) process for all generic drug approvals. The patent term extension bill that fell short of being enacted in the prior Congress was reintroduced in both the Senate and House. Waxman was setting the stage for a compromise in which some version of the patent term extension legislation would be enacted as part of a package that authorized ANDAs for generic drugs.

Waxman assigned two young lawyers on his Health Subcommittee staff, Bill Corr and John McLaughlin, to work with PhRMA and GPIA to see if an agreement could be reached on the parameters for extending drug patents. Peter Barton Hutt, a prominent Washington lawyer/lobbyist, and former FDA general counsel, represented PhRMA. He knew nothing about patent law but was assisted by a PhRMA patent committee that included lawyers from member companies. One of them was Alan Lourie of SmithKline, who later became a Federal Circuit Court of Appeals judge. I represented GPIA and was assisted by Jim Flug.

By the fall of 1983, I flew the Eastern Airlines Shuttle to DC weekly. Waxman's staff would function as go-betweens, presenting each side's patent proposals to the other and soliciting suggestions and language for possible compromises. Sometimes, we would meet as a group to hash out issues. Bill and John knew nothing about patent law and had to decide who seemed most credible as we worked through the issues. Congressman Waxman was a strong advocate for generic competition, so they were inclined to be sympathetic to my views if they seemed reasonable. I was fortunate to have Jim Flug by my side. Jim also didn't understand patent law but was very savvy about the legislative process and had great patience and wisdom. I would usually present my ideas to Jim first. That forced me to make them simple enough for Jim to understand before sharing them with Waxman's staff. Jim also helped me keep my worst adversarial instincts in check.

The patent term extension legislation that the Senate passed in 1982 would have allowed any patent claiming a drug subject to FDA review to be extended by up to seven years. That was far too generous. Brand name manufacturers had only presented evidence that the earliest patent claiming the chemical molecule that had never previously been approved as a drug was experiencing a loss of patent life before the FDA determined that it was safe and effective and could be approved for commercial use. My argument was simple: patent term extensions should only be available in that situation and only be granted for a single patent claiming the molecule or its approved medical use. Waxman and his staff agreed with that logic, and PhRMA's lawyers could not offer any reason to justify a broader extension.

As for the length of a patent term extension, I argued that the main reason that drugs do not get seventeen years of market monopoly is that they are not ready to be marketed on the day the earliest patent is granted. You don't have to prove that a drug is safe and effective to get a patent. You only need to show from a lab experiment or animal study that the chemical compound has a pharmacological property that might make it useful as a medicine. Product liability laws would prevent a responsible drug company from selling a drug without some proof that it was safe and effective, even if the FDA did not exist. It takes years of pre-clinical and human studies to determine if a drug is safe and effective. The patent time lost while those studies are done can't be blamed on the FDA since pharmaceutical companies don't even file for FDA approval before some of those studies are completed.

Important business reasons exist for filing a patent application long before a commercial product exists. Ownership of a patent is a prerequisite to making the investment necessary to commercialize a drug. It also discourages competitors from developing similar drugs. The brand name companies wanted to have their cake and eat it, too. They want to get patents long before a safe and effective drug exists and then blame the government for the shortened patent life that was their own doing.

Once Waxman and his staff understood these fundamentals, the question of how much of the lost patent time should be restored became a matter of negotiation. Eventually, we agreed that the maximum patent term extension would be five years, but no extension could extend the life of a patent for more than fourteen years from the date of FDA approval. The fourteen-year cap on extensions was understood to be a reasonable way to recognize that a patent owner should not be entitled to seventeen years of commercial monopoly if a drug was not ready for FDA approval when a patent was granted.

As for how to calculate the five-year extension, we agreed that only 50 percent of the time between the filing of an Investigational New Drug Application (IND) and the filing of a New Drug Application (NDA) would count toward an extension, but 100 percent of the time between the filing of the NDA and final FDA approval would be counted. This calculation also recognized that the applicant was responsible for some of the time it took to prove that a drug was safe and effective.

We had come a long way from the seven-year extension for every drug patent the Senate had approved. Only one patent would be eligible for a maximum extension of five years, but no extension would extend a patent for more than fourteen years from the FDA approval date. PhRMA's lawyers were not happy with the result. I had managed to separate need from greed in a way that satisfied Waxman and his team.

While the negotiations over the scope of patent term extensions were underway, I was closely monitoring patent litigation in the Eastern District of New York entitled *Roche v. Bolar*. Roche claimed that the formulation work required to apply for FDA approval of a generic drug was an act of patent infringement because it involved making and using the patented drug even though no sales were made until after the patent expired. If Roche prevailed, the commercial monopoly on a patented drug would not end when the patent expired. It would last until a generic manufacturer could formulate and test a competitive generic product, prepare and file an Abbreviated New Drug Application, and get FDA approval. That process would take at least two to three years after the patent expired.

Bolar undermined PhRMA's claim that the average monopoly was only eight years. It would be closer to eleven years before generic competition could begin if Roche successfully prevented all development work on a competitive generic drug until the patent expired. I told Waxman and his staff that PhRMA companies didn't have a case for any patent term extension, or at best, a significantly shorter one, if Roche prevailed. My argument caught PhRMA's lawyers by surprise. They offered no meaningful rebuttal but expressed the belief that Roche's argument was contrary to prevailing law and would be rejected by the court. Waxman felt misled because he had always assumed that generic competition would begin on the day the extended patent expired. We had reached an impasse.

In October 1983, the district court decided the *Bolar* case against Roche. The judge concluded that the experimental work to develop a generic drug for FDA approval before a patent expired was insignificant and did not give rise to a legitimate claim for patent infringement. The judge relied on a long line of precedents holding that minor, non-commercial uses of a patented invention were not actionable. Waxman's staff and the PhRMA lawyers were relieved. Under the *Bolar* decision, generic competition could begin on the day patents expired. The patent term extension provisions we had negotiated did not need to be changed. To everyone's amazement, I disagreed.

I was sure Roche would appeal the *Bolar* decision to the new Federal Circuit Court of Appeals. Congress created that court in 1982 to have exclusive jurisdiction over appeals from district court decisions in patent cases. I was one of a small group of New York patent lawyers who opposed the establishment of the Federal Circuit. We thought it would be biased in favor of patents. Therefore, I feared the Federal Circuit might reverse the *Bolar* decision. If that happened after Waxman's bill was enacted, brand name manufacturers would get a five-year patent extension and an extra three years of monopoly after their patents expired.

PhRMA's lawyers vigorously argued that my fears were not justified. They insisted that *Bolar* had been correctly decided and the appeal would fail. "In that case," I argued, "why don't we create certainty by including language in Waxman's bill that makes *Bolar* the law regardless of what the Federal Circuit may decide." It was a checkmate argument! Since PhRMA's lawyers had agreed that *Bolar* was correctly decided and generic competition should begin on the day a patent expired, they could not credibly refuse to put it in writing. It would not be long before they regretted taking that position.

I assumed that the agreements we had reached on patent term extension cleared the way for enacting Waxman's bill. So I felt blindsided when PhRMA's lawyers demanded that the legislation prohibit the FDA from approving any generic drug before the patents claiming the new drug had expired. It was an outrageous demand. While a patent is presumed valid as a matter of law, a party charged with patent infringement can assert that a patent is invalid and should never have been granted. It was well-known that the Patent Office granted many poor-quality patents that the courts eventually declared invalid. Generic drug manufacturers were entitled to the same right to contest the existence of a patent that every other industry enjoyed.

Federal courts are only obligated to hear cases involving real disputes, which means they are not obligated to decide whether a patent is valid unless there is a case of actual infringement. A drug patent could never be infringed unless the FDA first approved a generic version of a new drug. If the FDA were prohibited from doing so simply because a patent existed, there would be no legal pathway for challenging the validity of that patent. Drug patents would become incontestable, an absurd result from a public policy perspective.

While the law and common sense were on my side, politics were not. Pharmaceutical manufacturers had prior experience in several cases where a generic manufacturer deliberately infringed a drug patent but lacked the financial ability to pay damages. The Premo case, where my client was bankrupt, was an example. The abbreviated generic drug approval process could open the floodgates to widespread infringement of patents by insolvent manufacturers. Brand name drug companies needed a mechanism for preventing damaging commercial infringement of a valid patent. I had to find a reasonable solution to this problem.

A legal tool already existed—at least in theory. Courts can grant a preliminary injunction prohibiting commercial infringement if the evidence demonstrates that the patent owner will likely win and may suffer irreparable harm unless the infringement is immediately enjoined. The inability of a generic manufacturer to pay damages would satisfy the requirement for irreparable harm. I suggested to Waxman's staff that the legislation should prohibit the FDA from approving a generic drug for six months to give a patent owner time to ask a federal court for a preliminary injunction.

PhRMA's lawyers claimed my offer was disingenuous because courts rarely granted preliminary injunctions in patent cases. They were right. But I argued that if the courts were unwilling to prevent infringing sales before a patent was fully adjudicated, it made no sense for Congress to do so. PhRMA had no credible response. We needed a mechanism that allowed generic manufacturers to challenge the validity of low-quality patents while protecting brand name manufacturers from deliberate commercial infringement.

I found one. It would take the FDA up to two years to review and approve a generic drug application. Why not use that time to determine if a patent is valid? Generic drug manufacturers could contest the validity of drug patents without the risk of paying damages. Brand name manufacturers would maintain their monopoly unless the patent was first declared invalid. It seemed like a win-win idea.

I fleshed out a proposal for Waxman's staff. Brand name manufacturers would provide the FDA with a list of patents that claim the drug or the approved medical use of a drug they believed would be infringed if a generic version was approved. When an Abbreviated New Drug Application (ANDA) was filed, the generic manufacturer would certify that either (a) approval was being sought for the date on which the identified patents expire or (b) an earlier approval date was being sought because one or more of the listed patents was invalid or would not be infringed. If a patent was challenged, the generic applicant would serve the patent owner with written notice stating why the patent was invalid or not infringed. If the patent owner promptly filed a lawsuit, the FDA could not approve the generic application for eighteen months unless there was a judgment before then declaring the patent invalid or not infringed. The parties and the courts would agree to expedite the litigation so it would be completed within eighteen months. If the patent owner fails to sue, the FDA can approve the generic application immediately.

Brand name manufacturers were, in effect, getting an automatic preliminary injunction for eighteen months. It was an offer that PhRMA couldn't credibly refuse. It protected their patents against willful acts of infringement while giving generic manufacturers a reasonable pathway to challenging bad patents. Waxman's staff liked the proposal; PhRMA's lawyers were uncomfortable because their patents would likely receive greater scrutiny. But they were hard-pressed to find a credible reason to oppose the idea without admitting that their patents could not withstand that scrutiny.

In January 1984, an agreement in principle was announced after secret meetings between Waxman, Bill Haddad, and lobbyists for some of the largest pharmaceutical companies. The legislation would give patent term extensions to new drugs and provide an expedited approval process for generic drugs. It also guaranteed ten years of market exclusivity for all new drugs approved on or after January 1, 1982, assuring the new law would have minimal impact on pharmaceutical industry profits for at least a decade. Bill Haddad's private memo to the members of GPIA candidly pointed out that PhRMA didn't deserve any patent term extensions or other exemptions from competition. It was just the political price to be paid for getting the abbreviated new drug approval process enacted in the face of opposition from the powerful PhRMA lobby.

By mid-February, we were wrangling over the language of the tentative agreements that we had reached on patent term extensions, the *Bolar* exemption, and patent certification. Separately, Gene Pfiefer of King & Spaulding represented GPIA in working out the language of the abbreviated new drug approval process for generic drugs. The abbreviated approval process had been in place at the FDA for many years, and there was minimal controversy in translating that process into legislative language.

About that time, I was surprised by a call from Bill Haddad, who had Harold Snyder of Biocraft Laboratories on the call with him. Harold was the most patent-savvy member of the GPIA board. He told me the patent certification process was impractical. "Why would I spend $400,000 to challenge a patent if my generic competitors can get a free ride on my litigation expenses and enter the market on the same day that I do?" he argued. "Competition will drive down the price of the generic drug so fast that I won't be able to recover my litigation costs."

I immediately understood Harold's problem and asked him if he would feel differently if the first generic manufacturer to challenge a patent received a head start before competing generics could be approved. He liked that idea. We agreed on six months. Haddad dubbed it "the Snyder Amendment."

I proposed the Snyder Amendment to Waxman's staff and PhRMA's lawyers. There was no objection. That surprised me. I thought PhRMA would view the 180-day generic exclusivity as a bounty-hunting provision that would encourage patent challenges. They didn't see it that way, at least not initially. They seemed to believe that any delay in full generic competition would also delay the decline in the market share for the brand name drug and produce a net financial benefit. A few weeks later, I was in Bill Corr's office when he received a phone call from Lew Engman, the CEO of PhRMA. As he spoke, Bill gestured at me as if to say, "Lew is talking about you."

"What was that about?" I asked as he hung up the phone. Bill told me Lew and his team had second thoughts about the patent certification process. They feared I might personally use the certification process to embark on a campaign to attack the validity of pharmaceutical patents and accelerate generic competition. "Would you do that?" Corr asked.

"Until now, I have never given it a moment's thought," I said. "But it's a damned interesting idea." That off-hand conversation planted the first seed in my mind for the venture that would change my life.

Soon after, PhRMA's lawyers told Waxman's staff that the patent certification process had a fatal flaw. They claimed there would be no act of patent infringement that would force a federal court to take jurisdiction over a patent challenge. They were right! Because of the *Bolar* exemption, the formulation work required to seek FDA approval for a generic drug was no longer an act of patent infringement. The generic manufacturer's declaration of intent to challenge the validity of a patent was not an act of patent infringement since it did not involve making, using, or selling the patented product. A federal court would have the discretion to dismiss a patent infringement claim based on a patent certification because the patent had not yet been infringed. We were at another impasse.

I devised a convoluted but workable solution to the impasse by modifying the *Bolar* exemption. The *Bolar* exemption would only apply if a generic manufacturer sought approval to launch a generic drug after all identified patents had expired. If the generic applicant was filing a patent certification challenging one or more patents, the formulation work necessary to file the abbreviated new drug application would be an act of patent infringement.

In 1990, the US Supreme Court weighed in on the patent certification process created by Hatch-Waxman in deciding *Eli Lilly vs. Medtronic*. Justice Antonin Scalia described the clumsy language I used to fix the infringement problem as an inelegant piece of statutory draftsmanship. Fortunately, he agreed that it fixed the problem and was sufficient to compel federal courts to hear pharmaceutical patent challenges even though no commercial infringement had occurred. Given the pressure of trying to solve a complex problem, I took his insult as a compliment.

By early April 1984, a draft of the Waxman bill entitled "The Drug Price Competition and Patent Term Restoration Act of 1984" was made public. It included the patent term extension, *Bolar* exemption, and patent certification procedure proposals I had successfully negotiated. Senator Orrin Hatch (R-UT) agreed to be the principal sponsor of an identical Senate version of the legislation. The generic side immediately announced its support for the draft legislation. Under enormous pressure from Waxman and Hatch, PhRMA officially announced its support despite the opposition of several of its largest members. Lew Engman, PhRMA's CEO, felt he had no choice given that his legal team had agreed to all the patent provisions of the legislation after months of negotiation. A few days later, the Federal Circuit reversed *Bolar* and declared that formulating and testing a generic drug before a patent expired was an act of patent infringement. All hell broke loose!

My caution about the Federal Circuit had been vindicated. PhRMA's CEO and his legal team felt obliged to maintain their support for the Waxman draft. They had agreed to the *Bolar* exemption, knowing its only purpose was to nullify a decision by the Federal Circuit that would undermine the agreement on the length of patent term extensions. Ten of Pharma's largest members, including Pfizer, Bristol Myers, Johnson & Johnson, American Home Products, and Hoffman-La Roche, broke away and formed a dissident group to oppose the legislation. From their perspective, they were getting next to nothing out of the Waxman legislation. The maximum five-year patent term extension was offset by the loss of three years of post-patent monopoly that was wiped out by the *Bolar* exemption. The dissidents also viewed the patent certification process as a hunting license to challenge drug patents.

In June, hearings were held before the House and Senate Judiciary Committees. The dissidents claimed the *Bolar* exemption was an unconstitutional taking of their intellectual property rights. They brought in constitutional scholars Larry Tribe from Harvard and Norman Dorsen from NYU to make that case. But the Federal Circuit's decision acknowledged that Congress had the power to legislatively overrule its decision in *Bolar* and exempt the activities related to seeking FDA approval to market a generic drug from patent infringement claims. Many legislators were also uncomfortable with the idea that the dissidents wanted their monopolies to last longer than their patents. In the end, the constitutional arguments were unimpressive and went nowhere.

PhRMA also enlisted Gerald Mossinghoff, the head of the US Patent Office. Mossinghoff presented the committees with a highly complex chart and used it to argue that the limitations on the scope and length of patent term extensions were so complicated that it would be impossible for the Patent Office to implement them. It was a bad argument, but it turned out to be a great job interview. Less than a year later, Lew Engman was fired, and Mossinghoff became the new CEO of PhRMA.

By late August, the effort to reach an agreement with the dissident brand name companies was stalled. As the negotiations wore on, our side agreed to simplify the provisions of the patent term extension to make more patents eligible for the extension. The dissidents also convinced Senator Hatch to change the eighteen-month delay in FDA approval when a patent was challenged to thirty months. We did not resist the change. Generic manufacturers were not likely to begin competition before a patent was fully adjudicated out of fear that they would be liable for the patent owner's lost profits if an appellate court reversed a trial court finding that a patent was invalid. Therefore, a legislative time limit on the approval date for a generic drug was meaningless.

It was a presidential election year, and Congress was only a month away from adjournment. The prospect of getting any legislation enacted was slipping away. Senator Hatch pressured the dissidents to reach a compromise by suggesting the Senate would pass some version of the Waxman legislation with or without their support. Bill Haddad was negotiating with representatives of the dissidents by himself in an office in downtown DC. The dissident group was represented by Bill Ryan, legal counsel to Johnson & Johnson; Bill Greif, the senior lobbyist for Bristol Myers; and Alan Fox, a DC lawyer for Bristol Myers. It was a mismatch. Bill didn't know enough about the patent issues to negotiate alone, but he loved the attention he was getting. He would call me every few hours to discuss some new proposal from the dissidents that he didn't understand. We finally agreed that I should join the discussion, and I arrived in DC the next day.

The Orphan Drug Act, which had been recently enacted, contained a provision granting orphan drugs seven years of exclusivity without regard to patents. The dissidents were interested in a similar blanket exclusivity for all approved drugs. I suggested adding a provision to the Waxman bill prohibiting the FDA from accepting an application for a generic copy of any approved new drug based on a new chemical entity for five years. That would provide guaranteed market exclusivity for new drugs of about seven years, given the time needed to approve a generic application. The dissidents were surprised and delighted by my proposal. I didn't see it as being a major concession for several reasons. The main reason was that it was highly unlikely that many new drugs would have no patent protection. It also normally takes a couple of years before the market for a new drug becomes big enough to make a generic copy profitable. An independent source for the active ingredient will not likely be available before then. There was a large backlog of drugs with no patent protection and no generic competition. Generic manufacturers would be busy catching up for many years and would not suffer any economic hardship if a short window of exclusivity was created for new drugs.

The idea that every new drug would have market exclusivity for seven years gave the dissidents a victory of sufficient importance to justify their rebellion and bring the negotiations to a successful conclusion. To ensure that outcome, we also agreed to several two and three-year exclusivities for changes to a new drug in cases requiring new clinical studies. These exclusivities were more cosmetic than real since they did not prevent a generic applicant from immediately applying for approval to copy a change. They were not significantly longer than the time it would take a generic company to get FDA approval to copy the change if the exclusivity period did not exist.

Our agreement with the dissidents got immediate support from Senator Hatch. It infuriated Public Citizen and other consumer interest groups who characterized it as a "backroom" deal that ignored the public interest. Congressman Robert Kastenmeier (D.-WI) was irritated by the idea that we had created an unprecedented new monopoly outside of patent law. Henry Waxman was not consulted on the changes and was initially aligned with Public Citizen and Kastenmeier. Eventually, I convinced everyone, except Kastenmeier, that the additional non-patent exclusivities were not material.

The Drug Price Competition and Patent Term Restoration Act passed the Senate in late August by a vote of 99-0. Senator Howard Metzenbaum of Ohio abstained. Years later, he privately acknowledged to me that he regretted his vote. The House unanimously passed the bill in early September. On September 23, 1984, I sat in the Rose Garden with the leadership of the generic drug industry as President Ronald Reagan signed the Drug Price

Competition and Patent Term Restoration Act. It was one of the proudest moments of my life. We fundamentally changed the nature of competition between brand and generic drugs and ensured that low-cost versions of older medicines would be available to patients.

On the day the law was enacted, trade publications hailed the Waxman-Hatch Act as a landmark achievement. Henry's name deserved to be first. He had negotiated the initial compromise between the brand name and generic industries and overseen the complicated process of turning that compromise into legislation. Orrin Hatch became the Senate sponsor of the bill that Waxman and his team had negotiated and drafted. He deserved credit for his critical role in forcing the dissidents back to the negotiating table to get the legislation across the finish line. To patronize Hatch, the pharmaceutical lobby referred to the legislation as the Hatch-Waxman Act. That name stuck.

The press referred to Henry and Orrin as strange bedfellows—and they were. Henry was a classic liberal who favored consumers over corporations. Orrin was a "compassionate conservative" a generation before George W. Bush popularized that phrase. He grew up in Pittsburgh wearing a *mezuzah* (I never found out why) and became a bishop in the Mormon Church as an adult. Orrin believed that the big pharmaceutical companies were doing God's work. He and Bill Haddad formed a close friendship despite their vastly different political perspectives. Bill convinced Orrin that promoting the availability of generic drugs after patents expired was fair and would make Orrin a populist hero. He was right.

For all its complexity, the Hatch-Waxman Act was a negotiation to determine the price that would have to be paid to the big PhRMA companies in exchange for a new law expediting the FDA approval process for generic drugs. Neither Orrin nor Henry understood much about the complexities of patent law or the details of the disputes over *Bolar*, patent certification, or patent term extensions. They functioned like mediators in a conflict between the brand name and generic drug industries by listening to the arguments on each critical subject, asking questions, deciding who was credible, and twisting arms. Over time, Henry and Orrin relied on me to ensure that the price paid to PhRMA was not excessive. Orrin described me as "smart and tenacious" in remarks on the Senate floor in July 2002 when changes to Hatch-Waxman were being debated.

Henry complimented me for my "incomparable combination of intellect, vision, patience, and tenacity" in a letter he wrote when I was honored by the United Hospital Fund of New York in 1995. Both Henry and Orrin have described the Hatch-Waxman Act as the crowning achievement of their careers. I feel the same way. Few lawyers get the chance to play such a critical role in writing legislation that has an enormous impact on the lives of so many people.

Several months after the enactment of Hatch-Waxman, I participated in a public discussion with Peter Barton Hutt, the lead negotiator for PhRMA, to discuss how the legislation had evolved. I remember saying: "Generic Drug manufacturers make copies and cannot exist without a viable research-based drug industry that invents new drugs. My goal was not to kill the goose that lays the golden eggs but only to keep the goose from getting too fat." My clients would have paid almost any price in exchange for the abbreviated drug approval process, which was essential to their commercial viability. Most observers gave me credit for keeping the price down. I was fortunate to be in the right place at the right time and representing the right client. My pride in what I accomplished has always been tempered by the realization that, despite my best efforts, PhRMA still got far more than it deserved. An abbreviated process for approving generic drugs should have been enacted in the public interest without offsetting compensation to brand name drug companies. Instead, a dangerous principle was enshrined in the law. The pharmaceutical industry was not entitled to longer and stronger patent monopolies than any other industry in America. It was a bad idea. It has not led to greater biomedical innovation but has produced much higher costs for prescription medicines.

Chapter Five

CREATING THE PATENT CHALLENGE VENTURE

AMSTER & ROTHSTEIN HAD BECOME Amster, Rothstein & Engelberg. By 1984, the firm had more than twenty lawyers. Business was booming. But I was restless and thinking about the future. At age forty-five, I had difficulty seeing myself spending the next twenty years doing the same things I had done for the last twenty years. Maybe it was a mid-life crisis or the desire for more unique challenges like Hatch-Waxman, but I felt the need for change. I had no idea what would be next for me, but I felt a "next" was coming.

Not long after the Rose Garden ceremony, I began thinking about Bill Corr's telephone conversation with Lew Engman. Was there a viable business opportunity in exploiting Hatch-Waxman's patent certification process? Generic drug manufacturers lacked the financial resources or expertise to identify weak patents or the financial resources to challenge them. I had the knowhow and experience to fill that gap. Being the first manufacturer to market a generic version of an important new drug could be highly profitable. Perhaps I could partner with a generic manufacturer and share the risk and the profits. I would need a detailed strategy before starting such a venture. My partnership income put me in the ranks of Wall Street's best-paid lawyers. I couldn't just toss that away on a pipe dream.

I had folders of information about prescription drugs that I had accumulated over the prior decade. During the Christmas holidays of 1984, I began devising a plan for a venture at my kitchen table. What types of drug patents would be vulnerable? How long would it take to litigate a pharmaceutical patent? What kind of resources and experts would be needed? How large would the market for the branded drug need to be for the reward to make the risk worthwhile? Which generic manufacturers would be good partners? What kind of a profit-sharing deal could I make? I pondered these and many related questions. There was a lot to think about. By the time the holidays ended, I had filled a yellow legal pad with scribbled notes outlining my ideas.

I decided to focus on "me-too" drugs. Many commercially important drugs are copycat members of the same class, such as statins like Lipitor and Crestor or gastrointestinal drugs such as Prilosec and Nexium. A me-too drug is a chemical compound sufficiently similar in molecular structure to a known compound that it would be expected to have similar properties and uses. To be patentable, a me-too compound must have a new and unexpected property that the closely related known compound lacks. Otherwise, the law considers a me-too compound an obvious variant of a known compound that cannot be validly patented. My experience at Esso and the Justice Department provided me with expertise in the case law governing the determination of whether a new chemical compound meets the criteria for a valid patent.

Drug companies spend a lot of research money making minor molecular modifications to commercially successful products of their competitors in the hope of finding a drug with some difference that could be promoted to physicians to gain a share of the market. Often, they get patents on these products by making exaggerated, if not outright false, claims of superiority to the Patent Office. Patent examiners lack the skills and resources to evaluate this puffery and grant many patents that should never see the light of day.

Because of state laws that require substituting a lower-cost generic drug whenever one is available, the first generic competitor can quickly capture more than 90 percent of the market even though the discount from the branded drug's price is only 25–30 percent. That means that instead of making a profit of a penny or two per pill, the generic manufacturer might earn thirty or forty cents. With a six-month head start on a branded drug with annual sales of $100 million, a successful patent challenge could generate tens of millions in extra profits. I was confident that a small generic manufacturer would be happy to split that extra profit with a patent attorney willing to bear the legal cost of challenging a patent.

I decided that a patent would have to have five or six years of remaining patent life when the patent challenge began. It would take up to four years to complete the litigation and obtain FDA approval. If the patent was too close to its expiration date, other generic manufacturers would already be seeking FDA approval in anticipation of its expiration. That would shorten the head start for the first generic manufacturer and reduce the excess profit potential of a successful patent challenge.

With these criteria in mind, I turned my attention to the available lists of the top-selling prescription drugs. Three of the top-selling prescription drugs in 1984 were beta-blockers. I didn't know anything about beta-blockers. I quickly learned that Inderal, the first beta-blocker, was a critical drug for treating heart disease and hypertension. Its inventor won a Nobel Prize for the discovery. The beta-blockers discovered after Inderal were closely related in chemical structure and used for the same medicinal purpose. They were me-too drugs, although they were each commercially successful products. Did each possess some new and unexpected property that justified the patent grant? I doubted it. I decided to research Corgard (nadolol), Lopressor (metoprolol), and Tenormin (atenolol) to find a more definitive answer.

I have conducted dozens of patent validity studies over my twenty-five years in patent law. First, you read the patent and the history of proceedings at the Patent Office, which led the examiner to grant the patent. From that, you learn what the patent applicant and the examiner believed were the differences between the claimed invention and what was known earlier and which arguments were persuasive in the examiner's decision to grant a patent. Then, you hire a search firm specializing in patent and literature searches to look for prior patents and publications that might be more relevant than those considered by the patent examiner. Ultimately, you determine whether the new information from the search would have caused the examiner to refuse to grant the patent. You might also consult with experts in the field and get their opinion on whether the differences between what was known and what is claimed in the patent would have been obvious to a person of ordinary skill in the field.

In a radical departure from this established way of evaluating a patent, I postponed studying the beta-blocker patents or the history of proceedings in the Patent Office that led to the grant of those patents. I thought it would be better to learn what a skilled medicinal chemist would have known about beta-blockers at the time these me-too beta-blockers were discovered. Medical journals would disclose how the first beta-blockers were discovered, the pharmacological activity that made them useful, and the work done to optimize the desired pharmacological action or minimize side effects by varying the molecule's chemical structure. The medicinal chemists who invented Corgard, Lopressor, and Tenormin would certainly have used these published resources as their starting point to find a better beta-blocker. It would be rare for a patent examiner to study medical journals to gain a fundamental understanding of a class of drugs.

No patent search firm would take the time to develop the type of scientific history that I had in mind. I would have to do it myself, and I knew enough about organic chemistry and pharmacology to do it. Typically, this investigation into what the inventors knew and how they came to make the invention is the subject of document discovery and depositions after patent litigation begins. I couldn't afford to wait until then. I had to be confident in my chances of success before embarking on a risky new venture that could jeopardize my successful law practice.

There was no internet in those days. The best medical library was at the New York Academy of Medicine on 103rd Street in Manhattan. It was a late nineteenth-century building with an impressive medical library. When I could find the time, I would go to the Academy and search Index Medicus for review articles about the chemical structure and pharmacological activity of beta-blockers. After four or five two-hour trips to the library spread over a few months, I compiled about a dozen articles that traced the history of beta-blockers and the efforts to develop commercially valuable ones with desirable pharmacological properties. It was fascinating reading.

Here is what I learned. When the brain senses that you are about to engage in strenuous or stressful activity, it releases adrenaline. Adrenaline interacts with beta receptors located on the surfaces of every organ in the body. The interaction of adrenaline with the receptors signals the heart to pump harder and faster and the blood vessels to dilate so more oxygen and nutrients are delivered to the bloodstream. Picture a ship's captain sending a signal to the engine room of "all ahead full." For people with compromised heart muscles, this increased activity can cause pain in the heart called angina pectoris and sometimes can cause a heart attack. One idea for addressing the problem of overworking the heart was to block the beta receptors from interacting with adrenaline so the signal that causes the heart to do more work is never received. It would be like putting a governor on an engine to limit its top speed. That might cause a person to tire more quickly, but it could save their life by preventing a damaged heart muscle from overworking.

In the early 1960s, James Black synthesized the first beta-blockers. The earliest commercial beta-blocker was propranolol. It was sold under the brand name Inderal and was an enormous commercial success. It not only prevented angina but also reduced blood pressure for reasons that were not well understood. Black received a Nobel Prize in Medicine and was knighted for his discovery. Following Black's work, pharmaceutical companies worldwide began to make similar compounds, hoping to find a beta-blocker with better properties. A particular chemical structure, like a lock and key, was essential for blocking the beta receptors. Medicinal chemists understood which elements of the chemical structure were essential to the blocking function and what part of the molecule's peripheral structure might be changed to alter its pharmacologic properties without eliminating its ability to block the receptor.

Two pharmacological properties of beta-blockers were of particular interest to medicinal chemists. Some beta-blockers produced Intrinsic Sympathomimetic Activity (ISA), which meant that, to some degree, they mimicked the effect of adrenaline. Although the beta-blocker blocked adrenaline from interacting with the receptor, it produced the same effect as adrenaline but to a lesser degree. Whether some ISA was good or bad was an unresolved debate. The optimum amount of ISA might differ from patient to patient, depending on the severity of their heart condition. A beta-blocker with no ISA might be preferable for patients with more compromised heart conditions. For others, a modest amount of ISA might be preferred so the patient would not tire as quickly.

The second important property of a beta-blocker was the extent to which the beta-blocker molecule could be modified to make it more cardioselective. Beta receptors are present in many parts of the body, in addition to the heart. Stimulation of the beta receptors on the bronchial tubes causes vasoconstriction, which restricts oxygen flow to the lungs. Therefore, beta-blockers were not recommended for patients with asthma or other breathing problems. Medicinal chemists hoped to find a beta-blocker that selectively blocked the receptors of the heart but did not block the receptors located on the bronchial tubes. Some beta-blockers were a bit more selective than others. None were sufficiently selective to be helpful for those with breathing disorders. Dozens of beta-blockers were launched around the world following the introduction of Inderal. None exhibited any superior or unexpected properties. Some produced more ISA than others, while others were slightly more cardioselective, but there was nothing new or unexpected about the degree of change from one beta-blocker to another.

Armed with this background about beta-blockers, I was ready to study the Patent Office histories that led to the patents on Corgard, Lopressor, and Tenormin. I was shocked by what I learned. In each case, as expected, the patent examiner initially rejected the patent application because he determined that the beta-blocker claimed in the patent was a structurally obvious member of the class of compounds known to be useful as beta-blockers. In short, he concluded they were me-too drugs that were not patentable without proof that they possessed some superior or unexpected property. From what I had learned, the examiner was right.

Each patent applicant responded by claiming their beta-blocker possessed a superior or unexpected property. Experi-mental data was presented to show that it either had or lacked ISA compared to Inderal or was more cardioselective than Inderal. The patent examiner granted each of the patents based on these arguments.

None of these patents would have been granted if the patent examiner had been aware of the published medical literature about beta-blockers. He would have known that ISA and cardioselectivity were known properties of every beta-blocker. The fact that the compounds claimed in these patents had a little more or less of either of these properties was entirely expected and insufficient to make the compounds patentable. The sophisticated medicinal chemists at these major drug companies and their patent attorneys knew that ISA and cardioselectivity were well-known properties of beta-blockers and should have disclosed that knowledge to the examiner. If they had, these patents would never have been granted.

Although I was convinced I had the makings of a successful patent challenge, I am not a cardiologist. I wouldn't bet my career on the evidence I had found without a supporting opinion from a qualified cardiologist. My childhood friend and college roommate Saul Gitomer was a biostatistician and clinical monitor at Marion Laboratories, a pharmaceutical company in Kansas City. He worked with experts to get drugs approved by the FDA. I called Saul, explained what I was up to, and asked if he could help me find the right expert. Saul introduced me to Dr. Thomas Garvey, a consultant to the FDA with the perfect background for my needs.

Tom's livelihood depended on his relationships with big pharmaceutical companies. He was unwilling to be retained or go on record. As a favor to Saul, he agreed to read a memo I had written that summarized my findings and to meet with me to give me a verbal reaction. I met Tom for dinner near Dupont Circle in Washington. We had drinks and exchanged background stories before I asked him about my memo.

"They are going to have you killed," Tom said.

"Why?" I asked.

He said that my analysis of the beta-blockers was accurate and exposed the truth about how pharmaceutical companies develop me-too versions of important drugs. Tom verified that it was common for pharmaceutical companies to manipulate the structure of a known drug in the hope of finding a drug that was more potent or had fewer side effects. These me-too drugs were often launched even when they didn't materially differ from existing drugs for treating the same condition. They were still highly profitable because they were aggressively marketed. Tom had no expertise in patent law. But he confirmed that these beta-blockers resulted from routine modifications to the basic structure of known beta-blockers and did not possess any new or unexpected properties. He believed my challenge of the me-too beta-blocker patents might jeopardize the entire me-too business. It was just what I needed to hear. I was ready to move ahead and find a generic manufacturer to be my partner.

In the spring of 1985, I began talking to potential partners. Initially, I tested my idea on the owner of a small Canadian generic company. I did not tell him about the beta-blockers, just the general idea of challenging drug patents. He was enthusiastic and wanted to be my partner on whatever terms I wanted, although I had not made a business proposal. Given the small window to make large profits before other generic manufacturers entered the market, I thought I needed a domestic partner with robust distribution capabilities who could quickly penetrate the market if a patent challenge was successful.

The safest partner would be Rugby-Darby because it had the largest share of the generic drug market. The Ashkin family owned Darby, and Mike Ashkin, the founder's son, was the CEO. I knew him well since he was one of the founders of GPIA, the Generic Pharmaceutical Industry Association. He was flattered to have the first crack at making a deal with me. Of course, he immediately wanted to know what drugs I planned to challenge. I told him I would only disclose the drugs after we signed an agreement, but he could terminate the deal if his lawyers disapproved of my patent challenges. We quickly agreed on a fifty-fifty split of excess profits. Excess profits were defined as revenue above 150 percent of the cost to produce a pill, which was the industry's average gross margin on competitive products. If a pill cost two cents to manufacture, Darby would keep three cents, and we would split the difference between three cents and the actual selling price for as long as a difference existed or until the patent expired.

Unfortunately, Mike assigned the negotiations to one of his accounting executives who did not understand much about the substance of the arrangement and was overly concerned about controlling the cost of depositions, expert witnesses, transcripts, and other litigation costs. It made me uncomfortable. I was looking for a partner, and he treated me like a vendor. I put the negotiations with Darby on hold and went to see Jay Schein, the CEO of Henry Schein, Inc. Like Mike, Jay was the founder's son. The Schein and Ashkin families were bitter rivals for decades. Schein was a much smaller factor in the generic drug business. Schein owned Danbury Pharmacal and was building a new headquarters and factory for Danbury in Carmel, NY, less than ten minutes from my country home. That was a big plus.

Jay was enthusiastic about my proposal and immediately accepted my terms. He also offered me an additional $250,000/year to serve as an advisor to Schein and Danbury on all matters related to Hatch-Waxman and generic drugs. I could continue to represent the generic trade association and maintain my law practice with the understanding that the patent challenges and advising Schein would be my primary focus. The offer was too good to be true. The deal would give me enough income to focus on the patent challenges I had identified and look for additional challenges. How I would work things out with my law partners was unclear, but I didn't care. Even if I gave up my law practice, I had no downside.

I drafted a formal agreement, and Jay signed it without having it reviewed by his lawyers. Shortly after, Richard Goldberg, Jay's corporate counsel and trusted confidante, invited me to lunch. Richard asked me how much money I expected to earn under the agreement. I told him I had no idea whether it would be two cents or $200 million. He suggested we pick a number and add a cap to the agreement. I refused to discuss it. I didn't have a financial goal and would not be limited by one. It would still be a great deal for both parties, even if my share was astronomical. Richard and I began a friendship that day that lasted until his death more than thirty-five years later. We often reminisced and laughed about that first meeting. I always admired him for his charming but persistent effort to protect a client he thought had failed to protect himself.

The deal with Schein was contingent on an independent review of the patent challenges, which I would disclose after signing the agreement. If Schein's lawyers disagreed with my plans, Schein would have sixty days to terminate. I vividly remember the meeting at Schein headquarters when I first disclosed the beta-blocker challenges. Jay was there along with Marty Sperber, the Executive VP of Schein; Stan Bergman, the chief financial officer; Nessim Maleh, the CEO of Danbury Pharmacal; and Bill Haddad, who had given up his position as CEO of the GPIA to become an executive at Danbury. Everyone except Stan Bergman, who now runs Schein, was flabbergasted by the audacity of my proposal to challenge the beta-blocker patents. Stan bluntly stated, "This is the craziest scheme I have ever heard in my life. You can't seriously believe that you can take on the largest pharmaceutical manufacturers in the world and win."

"Yes, I do," I replied.

My law partners were unaware of my efforts to create a venture to challenge drug patents. When the Schein agreement was ready to be signed, I met with them to explain my plan and share the details of the Schein contract. I explained that I intended to complete my work on pending matters but would no longer take on new clients, take responsibility for new litigations, or play any significant role in firm management. Given my reduced role, I would give up my share of the partnership profits. My income would come solely from the Schein retainer and any hours I spent on firm matters. No partner or associate would be required to work for Schein without payment at normal hourly rates, but the firm would receive 20 percent of the payments I received from successful patent challenges. Economically, it was a big win for my partners.

They were stunned by the proposal, and there was no instant response. We met many times in the days after I dropped my bombshell, and they also met without me. Everyone acknowledged that my proposal would significantly increase their incomes in the short term and could produce a windfall if my venture succeeded. But they did not want me to sign the Schein agreement. The firm was enormously successful, and I was essential to that success. They would have to hire more young lawyers and work much harder without my daily involvement.

Eventually, my partners agreed to accept the arrangement, but only if I formally resigned from my partnership and became "of counsel" to the firm. It meant that my name would be removed from the firm letterhead, and a formal announcement of my change in status would be sent to all clients. It was a stupid idea. I couldn't tell whether the proposal was intended to force me to resign or to abandon the venture. It didn't matter. My only reason for staying was to preserve the firm's continuity and provide a fallback position for myself if the venture failed. That would be impossible if the firm announced a change in my status. I would have to explain it to my clients. They would feel abandoned, and most would walk away. "This doesn't make sense," I said. "If my name goes off the door, I go out the door."

I felt a sense of relief. In truth, leaving the firm was the wisest decision. It would free me to focus on the patent challenge venture without distractions. I was forty-six years old and had built a solid reputation. There would be plenty of offers from general practice firms to start new practices in intellectual property law. I could afford to spend four or five years on the Schein venture and still be able to rebuild my law practice if the venture failed. But it still felt like I was jumping off a cliff.

The formal announcement of my resignation was made public on December 31, 1985. I agreed to stay on informally for an indefinite period to complete a few matters of importance to clients and try to convince some of them to remain clients of the firm. It took only a few months to accomplish that. I remained on good terms with my former partners, and my close personal relationship with Mort Amster continued for many years. I said my final goodbyes to the firm in a one-sentence speech at the annual office Christmas party in 1986, stating, "I joined this firm seventeen years ago, and my patent has expired."

Chapter Six

DRUG PATENT LITIGATIONS—THE BEGINNING

The months I spent at the Amster firm after my resignation were depressing. I went from being at the center of the daily action at the firm to being an outsider and avoiding contact with everyone other than my secretary. That led me to spend my free time at The Chemists' Club, around the corner from the office. It had a small library with a good collection of books on medicinal chemistry. One of the drugs on my original list of potential patent challenges, other than the three beta-blockers, was Flexeril (cyclobenzaprine). It was a popular muscle relaxant sold by Merck for treating lower back muscle spasms. The drug had originally attracted my attention because the patent did not claim the drug molecule but only its use as a muscle relaxant. That usually meant the molecule wasn't new and could not be patented.

I studied the patent and confirmed that cyclobenzaprine, the active ingredient, had been disclosed to be useful as a tranquilizer in prior patents. The compound was almost identical to amitriptyline in molecular structure. Amitriptyline was the active ingredient in Elavil, an enormously successful Merck tranquilizer. Was amitriptyline also known to be useful as a muscle relaxant, or was this a new and unexpected property of cyclobenzaprine? I knew from prior experience relating to the patenting of chemical compounds that the Flexeril patent was invalid if muscle relaxation was a known property of amitriptyline. Amitriptyline was such a well-known and widely studied drug that medical journals would have disclosed its muscle relaxant capability if it existed.

The first book I pulled from the shelf at The Chemists' Club was a medicinal chemistry textbook that included a chapter entitled "Muscle Relaxants." The chapter was authored by Edward Engelhardt, the Merck chemist who invented amitriptyline. That alone made the chapter worth while. I sat down on the floor between the stacks and started reading. Suddenly, there it was! An unambiguous statement by Engelhardt that an article by Sinha and others published in the *Japan Journal of Pharmacology* (1966) disclosed that amitriptyline was a muscle relaxant. Engelhardt had written this book chapter before Merck filed the patent application claiming cyclobenzaprine as a muscle relaxant.

Within a few weeks, I obtained a copy of the official proceedings in the Patent Office that led the patent examiner to grant the cyclobenzaprine patent. Merck had not only failed to disclose the Japanese article acknowledging that amitriptyline was a known muscle relaxant but had told the Patent Examiner that amitriptyline had no muscle relaxant capability. It was a flat-out lie! More than a decade earlier, in the *Sea Lark* case, I successfully got the Penn Yan patent declared unenforceable in similar circumstances involving misrepresentations made to the patent examiner to procure a patent. A court can refuse to enforce a patent for inequitable conduct if an applicant deliberately withholds or misrepresents information that would have been material to the examiner's decision to grant it.

After only a few hours of effort, I had documented a slam dunk case against Merck's Flexeril patent. I instructed Schein to develop a generic version of cyclobenzaprine for submission to the FDA.

By the spring of 1985, I momentarily felt like I had retired. Danbury was preparing Abbreviated New Drug Applications for cyclobenzaprine and the three beta-blockers. It would be at least a year until those applications were filed and the patent challenges could begin. I had nothing to do except prepare those cases for trial. I didn't need a formal office, secretary, or legal associates. Paperwork would be minimal until lawsuits began. I got into a routine of spending two days a week at the medical libraries in New York doing research and the remainder of my time at my weekend home in Carmel reading and writing. I bought a Compaq "portable" computer that weighed twenty-eight pounds and transported it to the city every week in the trunk of my car. I learned to use WordStar word processing software and became a proficient hunt-and-peck typist. I loved the freedom of working at home. My home office included a stationary bike for exercise breaks and a hot tub immediately outside the door for relaxation breaks. My work clothes were a T-shirt and a pair of gym shorts, a dress code that continues until now. Thirty-five years later, when COVID-19 struck, everyone adapted to my lifestyle and began to appreciate how productive it can be to work at home.

I worked for many uninterrupted hours—far more time than I had ever put in at the law firm. The first lawsuits did not formally begin until early 1987; the first trial was in February 1988. By then, I had spent thousands of hours preparing for the trial. I had considered every move and countermove that might impact the outcome and studied everything written about these drugs. Mel Van Woert, my expert witness in the Flexeril case, once remarked that I could have taught his medical school pharmacology class. Most lawyers in busy practices don't have the time to focus on one or two cases with the intensity that I did, and their clients would never pay for it. It gave me an overwhelming advantage over opposing counsel, even though they outnumbered me. You can't make up for a deficit in your depth of knowledge about a case by adding more lawyers; spreading responsibility makes it worse.

I described the intensity with which I had prepared my cases when I was a panelist at a patent law educational seminar on contingent fee patent litigation in Hilton Head in the early 1990s. An audience member asked: "What would be your advice to a pharmaceutical company trying to win a case against you?"

"Focus!" I responded without hesitation. "Limit the staffing to one or two lawyers and pay them double their normal hourly rate if they promise to work on your case and nothing else."

During this period of intense preparation, I made several decisions about presenting my cases that were critical to my success. The first decision was to ensure that the cases were tried before a judge without a jury. By the mid-1980s, most patent cases were tried before juries. Juries were far more prone to uphold patents, especially in cases where the patent covered a commercially successful product. In a patent challenge under the Hatch-Waxman Act, there was no commercial infringement and no possibility that the patent owner could recover any monetary damages. The only issue was whether an injunction should be granted to prevent the challenger from selling a generic copy before the patent expired. A long line of legal precedents established that a party seeking an injunction as the sole remedy is not entitled to a jury. I would insist that the trial court follow those precedents and deny a jury.

In a typical patent infringement trial, the patent owner presents evidence first. Usually, the first two weeks of the trial are an elaborate show-and-tell in which witnesses present evidence about the debilitating impact of some medical condition, how drug company scientists spent many years and billions of dollars and endured many failures before the patented drug was discovered, the rigorous clinical trials that were conducted to assure the safety and efficacy of the drug, and how the drug has served to provide relief for millions of patients and earn billions of dollars for the company. By then, the judge or jury tends to be biased toward the patent owner and sees the infringer's assertion that the patent is invalid as a weak excuse for trying to profit from the patent owner's innovative efforts.

The elaborate and highly prejudicial show-and-tell is eliminated at a trial where the infringer presents evidence first. The judge's first impression of the merits of the patent is acquired through the eyes of the infringer. The court immediately learns that the patent claims subject matter that is, at best, only modestly different from what was known and that the patent would never have been granted if the patent examiner had been aware of the evidence presented by the infringer bearing on the patent's invalidity. That makes the judge anxious to hear the patent owner's response to the central issues in the case presented by the infringer. Judges don't have the time or patience to listen to an elaborate but irrelevant presentation regarding the history of a drug that is not directly responsive to the case for invalidity made by the infringer. Flipping the order in which the evidence is presented shortens a trial by focusing on why the patent should not have been granted rather than why it was granted.

The patent owner has the burden of proving infringement, and the alleged infringer has the burden of proving invalidity. The party with the burden of proof has the right to present evidence first. Since my client would be copying an FDA-approved drug, it made sense to admit infringement so that I could present evidence first at the trial.

It was also conventional practice in patent litigation for a party seeking to invalidate a patent to throw the kitchen sink at an opponent and present every technical flaw as a reason to declare the patent invalid. Most attorneys don't present a streamlined case because they fear their clients may accuse them of lacking thoroughness. I strongly felt that limiting a case to the best one or two reasons the patent was invalid would produce clarity and confidence. It would enable me to present my case in a day or two of trial. Judges appreciated that approach, and patent owners feared it. It made the case against the patent easier for the judge to understand, and it limited the ability of the patent owner to clutter the record with a mountain of irrelevant material designed to deflect a court's attention away from the central issue.

Most lawyers also try to withhold evidence and strategy until the last moment, hoping to surprise their opponent. I took the opposite approach and presented my entire case in the patent certification notice before the litigation started. The Hatch-Waxman Act states that when a generic applicant notifies the FDA of its intention to challenge a patent, the challenger must provide the patent owner with a written statement of the reasons for the patent challenge. But the law does not demand any degree of specificity. My challenge document looked like a post-trial brief, which presented the relevant facts, the supporting documents, and the legal arguments as to why those facts made the patent invalid. It gave my case a positive first impression with the trial judge by letting him know there was a serious basis for the patent challenge. It also dramatically limited the ability of my opponents to harass me with irrelevant requests for pretrial discovery. When discovery was sought, I could waive the patent challenge notice at the judge and confidently say that it contained all the evidence we intended to present at the trial. There was nothing left for the patent owner to discover except to conduct a pretrial examination of my expert witnesses.

I was working alone without any other lawyers, paralegals, or secretaries. My game plan enabled me to keep the cases simple. At the first conference with the trial judge, I would point out that this was a Hatch-Waxman case, no damages were possible, and request confirmation that the patent owner was not entitled to a jury. I would then admit patent infringement and ask the judge to rule that the patent challenger would go first at trial because we had the burden of proof on patent validity. Finally, I would call the judge's attention to our detailed patent challenge notice, note that we had eliminated the need for significant pretrial discovery, and demand an expedited trial date was required by the Hatch-Waxman Act. My opponents were blindsided. It created the appearance that the patent was very weak. First impressions matter.

Hiring expert witnesses turned out to be much more challenging than I expected. Large pharmaceutical companies maintain important financial relationships with academic medical centers. The academics with the best credentials are reluctant to oppose the industry's interests out of fear that grant money will dry up. With persistence and luck, I found two highly qualified experts for the beta-blocker cases. Dr. Bernard Love had a PhD in chemistry and had worked as a medicinal chemist for SmithKline and others. He had specific experience studying the impact of structural changes to the beta-blocker molecule on its pharmacological activity. Dr. Udho Thadani was a Professor of Medicine at the University of Oklahoma and Vice Chief of the Section of Cardiology. He had experience, dating to 1969, in evaluating beta-blockers in treating angina pectoris and hypertension as a research fellow in the UK. Dr. Melvin Van Woert was a Professor of Neuropharmacology at Mount Sinai in New York with impressive research credentials in central nervous system drugs. He was well-qualified to discuss the pharmacology of cyclobenzaprine and amitriptyline.

Danbury filed its Abbreviated New Drug Applications for Squibb's Corgard beta-blocker and Merck's Flexeril muscle relaxant in late 1986 and Ciba-Geigy's Lopressor beta-blocker a few months later. The application for ICI's Tenormin beta-blocker was delayed because Danbury could not find a source for the active ingredient. My detailed patent challenge notices were ready, and my experts were on board. I was ready—or so I thought. In truth, I wasn't mentally prepared to manage three major litigations simultaneously.

My opponents were three of the largest patent firms in New York. They were accustomed to cutting loose an army of young partners and associates to inundate the early stages of litigation with a continuing barrage of document requests, interrogatories, deposition requests, and procedural motions. It was time-consuming and meaningless because there was nothing to discover. No executive of Danbury had ever read the patents or participated in preparing the certification notice. My opponents were unsatisfied with that answer and wanted access to my notes and thought process. They even tried to depose me, get access to drafts of my patent challenge notice, and delve into my thought processes and work product. In the end, no judge allowed them to do so. They only had the usual opportunity to depose my expert witnesses before trial. But dealing with the discovery process in three cases simultaneously was time-consuming and exhausting.

Pretrial discovery was critical to my trial strategy. I wanted to delve into the events leading to filing for each patent to find evidence that the inventors knew the same things I had learned from the medical literature and hid that knowledge from the Patent Office. In the beta-blocker cases, I expected to find evidence that the inventors knew that ISA and cardioselectivity were well-known pharmacological properties of all beta-blockers and that their arguments to the contrary in proceedings before the Patent Office were false. In the Flexeril case, I was looking for direct evidence that Dr. Engelhardt had shared his knowledge that amitriptyline was a muscle relaxant with other Merck employees and patent lawyers, and they deliberately withheld that information from the patent examiner.

Merck put me in a room full of filing cabinets that contained hundreds of thousands of documents related to the development of Flexeril. They knew I was working alone and hoped I would never get through all the documents and find what I was looking for. To their amazement, I finished my review in a few hours. Most of the file drawers contained communications with the FDA or clinical trial information dated long after the patent was granted and were irrelevant. The only documents of interest to me would be dated before Merck filed its patent application. By scanning the content of files for document dates, I quickly found the single drawer that contained the documents I sought. Minutes after that, I found the smoking gun. A handful of memos and correspondence showed that Merck knew that amitriptyline had been disclosed as a muscle relaxant in the 1966 Japan pharmacology journal and that the disclosure would prevent the grant of a patent. The documents proved that Merck deliberately suppressed what they knew and made arguments to the patent examiner contrary to their knowledge. My heart raced as I made detailed notes about those documents in case Merck refused to produce copies. I was confident this evidence would doom Merck's patent.

The Flexeril and Corgard cases were filed in Delaware and assigned to Judge Murray Schwartz. In the fall of 1987, he set a schedule that would force me to try the Flexeril case in early February and the Corgard case in mid-March. Given all the requirements for formally submitting evidence and briefs before and after the trial, I would have to work around-the-clock for six months. Judge Schwartz was deliberately testing me. He understood that the timing of these lawsuits had been up to me, and he would not show me any mercy. It was far too late in the game to bring in any help. Educating and supervising them would take longer than it was worth. I would have to face the reality of working eighteen hours a day and hope for the best.

I planned to present the entire Flexeril case through the testimony of a single expert witness, Melvin Van Woert, and the hostile cross-examination of Merck employees. I still have nightmares about preparing Mel to testify during the week before the trial. Mel was a good scientist with outstanding credentials but a very laid-back character. He had never been an expert witness and didn't understand what to expect. We worked many hours daily to prepare a script for his direct testimony. I was focused on giving him a feeling for the atmosphere he would encounter in the courtroom and how we would try to educate the judge about the issues the judge would have to decide. I explained that although I would be asking him questions, I intended it to feel like a conversation in which broad questions would enable him to give answers as though he was teaching a course to a student with little background in the subject matter. His job was to teach the court what was already known about cyclobenzaprine and amitriptyline as antidepressants and muscle relaxants and make it clear that muscle relaxation was not a new or unexpected property of this class of compounds. Mel didn't get it. During our rehearsals, he left out critical facts and became bewildered when I asked follow-up questions to elicit them.

I also spent countless hours cross-examining Mel. He was going to be cross-examined at trial by Joe Fitzpatrick, one of the best patent trial lawyers in the business. I went through every line of questioning Joe might use to shake Mel's credibility and pleaded with him not to become combative or hostile. My final words to Mel were to stay calm and stick to the basics. "Let me be the advocate," I cautioned. "You don't have to say 'no' to every question Joe may ask. We don't have to have every fact resolved in our favor. If you sound reasonable, you will be far more credible." I went to bed the night before the trial feeling that I had foolishly bet my career on a single witness who didn't understand his role.

When I arrived in the courtroom for the start of the trial, I was surprised to see a full gallery. In addition to a crowd from Merck, dozens of lawyers from the Corgard and Lopressor cases were present. Everyone was there to see how I would do against Joe Fitzpatrick and his team and to get a preview of what to expect when their cases came to trial. I was alone at my table, surrounded by boxes of documents, deposition transcripts, and notebooks containing thousands of pages of evidence. It appeared to the assembled audience that David was about to battle with Goliath. I was calm. The moment before I would rise to speak at a trial or appellate argument was always a moment of calm for me. That inner peace came from a belief that there was nothing more I could have done to prepare and the confidence that would be good enough.

I knew Joe Fitzpatrick well because I had served on the New York Bar Association Patent Committee for several years while he was the chair. Joe was a brilliant lawyer and a quick study, but he was in for a surprise. I intended to conduct the trial at breakneck speed. Joe had not attended a single pretrial meeting or deposition. He would be relying on his lieutenants to keep him up to speed; there would not be enough time to do that. Joe was expecting a trial that would last at least two weeks. I expected to finish in less than five days.

After a brief opening statement, I called Mel to the stand. It could not have gone more smoothly. We broke for lunch after less than three hours, but my presentation was almost complete. I decided to wrap things up right after lunch so that Fitzpatrick would have to begin his cross-examination immediately and spend several hours with the witness before we adjourned for the day. He wouldn't be ready for that, giving Mel an advantage.

Fitzpatrick's cross-examination proceeded just as I had predicted. There was not a single line of questioning that caught Mel by surprise. You could see Mel's confidence growing with each question from the sound of his voice and his body language. He was calm, articulate, and agreeable but held his ground. It was an outstanding performance. Fitzpatrick struggled to keep the cross-examination going to the end of the day so he could regroup with his team that evening, hoping to conduct a more impactful cross-examination the next morning.

Mel and I had dinner that night. He was happy and excited. "How can anyone ever beat you?" he said. "You anticipated everything that would happen in that courtroom. All the things you told me happened just as you described them. I finally understood what our preparation was about. It was amazing and fun."

I thanked Mel but cautioned him not to get too cocky. "They will be working all night to devise a way to dent your testimony," I told him. "You still have a tough couple of hours ahead." Mel continued to perform well the next day.

When we returned from lunch after Mel's cross-examination ended, I told the court I had no further witnesses. It was another surprise blow to Fitzpatrick. He was not expecting to start calling Merck's witnesses so quickly and was completely off balance. From Tuesday afternoon and the rest of the week, Merck called nine witnesses to try and refute my case. I had pages of cross-examination questions prepared for each witness that were keyed to documents and pages in their pretrial depositions. Nothing these witnesses said at the trial surprised me. I could pounce on every prior inconsistent statement and severely damage the credibility of each witness. And because I was so immersed in the details, I moved at lightning speed, which made the cross-examinations more impactful and gave Fitzpatrick and his team little time to rehabilitate his witnesses or prepare for the next witness.

It was an exhausting week. I got little sleep. I would meet with Mel immediately after the trial ended each day to get his notes and impressions about the testimony given and then take a break for a drink and dinner. Based on that day's testimony, I updated my cross-examination notes from about 8 p.m. to midnight. As soon as my head hit the pillow, my mind went into instant replay. I spent most of the night replaying the trial. Fortunately, as I planned, the trial ended after lunch on Friday. Joe Fitzpatrick walked across the courtroom to shake my hand. He said: "Al, if I hadn't seen it for myself, I wouldn't believe anyone could try a case like this alone. You did a great job." I thanked him for his kind words. I could tell from his body language and tone that he felt defeated. The outcome would not be known for at least six months. I was confident I had won.

There was no time to rest. The Squibb Corgard trial was five weeks away. I had been preparing the beta-blocker cases for almost three years and knew I would be ready. My opponents were in chaos. Jerry Lee of Morgan & Finnegan represented Squibb. Jerry was more of a politician than a trial lawyer. He was always polite and patronizing, but he lacked the killer instinct of the best trial lawyers I had encountered. Jerry had been president of both the New York Patent Law Association and the American Patent Law Association. John Vassil, one of Jerry's more pugnacious partners, initially acted as lead counsel for Squibb, and Jerry played almost no role in the early stages of trial preparation. About two months before the trial, Vassil withdrew because of an emergency for another client, and the senior associate on the case took maternity leave. Jerry had to step in with a new team at the last minute. He was in over his head and knew it. Jerry had also been in the courtroom for the Flexeril trial and was worried about his ability to cope with the speed at which I had presented evidence to keep Joe Fitzpatrick off balance.

Less than two weeks after the Flexeril trial, Jerry called and requested a formal meeting with the senior management of Squibb at their Princeton campus to discuss settlement. It had never occurred to me that settlement was a possibility. It was not like the Premo case, where I was rescuing a client from bankruptcy who was willing to accept a small payment that was less than the cost of conducting a trial. A settlement would require a payment of millions of dollars, not some token amount.

Nevertheless, my agreement with Schein had anticipated the possibility of settlement and called for a fifty-fifty split.

The stakes were far too high. I was too personally involved to handle this negotiation alone. Jay Schein assembled a team for the settlement meeting that included Marty Sperber, Jay's second-in-command, Richard Goldberg, his outside counsel, and me. We made a grand entrance to the Squibb campus in Princeton in the longest stretch limo we could find. The meeting was led by Squibb's executive vice president, who was surrounded by several other executives and lawyers. After some posturing, Squibb finally offered $1 million in cash and an additional $10 million from a five-year manufacturing arrangement in which Danbury would produce drugs for Squibb at a guaranteed net profit of $2 million/year. Squibb would have the option to pay the $2 million each year for five years instead of doing any business with Danbury. The manufacturing arrangement was a fig leaf designed to make a cash settlement look like a business deal rather than a payoff to avoid a trial.

We asked for a private room to discuss the offer. We were giddy! For Danbury, $5.5 million was far more money than the total profits the company had earned over its entire existence. For Schein, it was almost as much as they had paid to acquire Danbury. It was more than what I could earn from practicing law for a decade. We called Jay and got his blessing to accept the offer.

When we returned to the conference room, Squibb's executive vice president said, "There is no deal until I meet alone with Mr. Engelberg." With consent from my side, I went into a private meeting.

The EVP was blunt. "We want to retain you to review the patents on our pipeline of new drugs and will pay you $100,000 for five days of work. You won't make any notes or write about anything you review without our consent except acknowledging that you conducted the review."

I smiled and said, "Basically, you want to create a conflict of interest for me so that I won't be able to challenge another Squibb patent."

"Exactly," he answered. "We don't ever want to see you again." It was a flattering tribute.

I told the EVP I would need Schein's consent before accepting his offer. Marty Sperber's response was predictable: "We are entitled to half the $100,000 fee."

Squibb had no idea I was working on a contingent fee arrangement and would get 50 percent of the settlement. As we left their headquarters, their in-house patent lawyer pulled me aside and said, "You must be disappointed. We will never know who was right about the patent's validity."

I grinned and said, "Not at all. I am confident I was right. I couldn't care less what the judge thinks."

Our limo left the Squibb campus and pulled into the driveway of a Marriott Hotel just outside of Squibb's headquarters. We went into the bar, got three quart containers of vodka on the rocks, and piled back into the limo for the drive back to New York. It was a joyous ride. I was free of the physical and mental burden of back-to-back trials and felt rich.

Within a couple of months, I completed the post-trial briefs in the Flexeril case and was temporarily out of work. The trial of the next beta-blocker case was over a year away. I was free to recharge my batteries and enjoy the summer. Life could not have been better. The Squibb settlement began a new chapter in life for my wife Jane and me. Unfortunately, her battle with Hodgkin's lymphoma had become active again. Then, by June, after another round of chemotherapy, she was in remission again, and the treatments had stopped. We spent the summer playing golf, sailing, and entertaining friends and family. We spent the last weekend in August at a reunion with our oldest and closest college friends.

The morning after the reunion, Jane woke up feeling sick. By nightfall, she was dead. It was septic shock. Her immune system was compromised from years of chemotherapy and radiation treatments. A bacterial infection shut down her vital organs with incredible speed. We always knew Jane would not make it to old age, but we never discussed it. After eighteen years of enduring treatment and fighting for a normal life, suffering through a lingering decline to death would have been unbearable for both of us. In hindsight, sudden death was a blessing, even though we never had a chance to say goodbye.

As I returned home from Jane's funeral two days later to begin sitting shiva, the phone rang. It was Joe Fitzpatrick, Merck's lead attorney in the Flexeril case. "Al," he said. "Congratulations!"

"Congratulations?" I responded, choking back tears. "I just buried my wife."

Joe was a kind man and was very apologetic. "I had no idea," he said. "I assumed you knew Judge Schwartz released his decision today, and you won."

I completely broke down. It was the greatest victory of my life, and the only person I wanted to share that moment with was gone. From the time I left my law firm in 1985, I had been living a life of solitude in which I was focused—often for eighteen hours a day—on making a success of the Schein venture. I never felt lonely. Jane was always there for me—sharing meals, going for walks, playing golf, and discussing hopes, fears, and the stories of everyday living. How would I function without her constant support and companionship? I had no answer.

Chapter Seven

DRUG PATENT LITIGATIONS—THE END

AFTER TAKING A COUPLE MONTHS to mourn, and with the support of family and friends, I began life again and tried to find a balance between work and the need to restart my life. Fortunately, the next beta-blocker trial was nine months away. My only immediate task was to write a brief and prepare for an oral argument on Merck's appeal of the Flexeril decision.

Judge Schwartz's decision in the Flexeril case (*Merck v. Danbury Pharmacal*, 694 F.Supp.1 (D. Del 1988)) held that Merck's witnesses were not credible and that Merck was guilty of withholding information from the patent examiner that may have caused him to deny the patent. He concluded that Merck was guilty of inequitable conduct in procuring the Flexeril patent, the patent was unenforceable, and Schein (Danbury) was entitled to recover its legal fees and costs. I called Joe Fitzpatrick to explain that I had no billing records and that we would have to find another way of determining the legal fees to which Danbury was entitled. I proposed a settlement payment of $400,000 and suggested that if Merck refused, I would conduct discovery as to how much Merck had spent on the case as proof of the amount that would be reasonable. Merck probably spent well over $1 million. They swiftly accepted my proposal without further negotiation.

Merck appealed Judge Schwartz's decision to the Federal Circuit Court of Appeals. There was a chance they could win because Judge Schwartz had ruled that the patent was valid even though it was unenforceable. Those two conclusions would seem incompatible to anyone other than a patent attorney. Patent law requires clear and convincing evidence to overturn the presumption that a patent granted by the Patent Office is valid. In contrast, a patent examiner's decision to grant or deny a patent is based on a preponderance of the evidence, which is a much lower standard. Because of this difference in the standard of proof, Judge Schwartz found that the same evidence that was sufficient to support a conclusion that the examiner might never have granted the patent was also insufficient to overcome the presumption of validity once a patent was granted. It was a technically correct but absurd decision that left Merck free to argue that its misrepresentations were immaterial because they were insufficient to invalidate the patent. Fortunately, that argument was contrary to legal precedent.

The Flexeril appeal coincided with a time in which many large corporations and patent bar associations were lobbying for a change in the law to make it more difficult for courts to hold patents unenforceable. They wanted a no harm, no foul rule, meaning that if information withheld from a patent examiner was insufficient to make a patent invalid, then it should also be insufficient for a finding that there was inequitable conduct in withholding that information.

Judge Schwartz's Flexeril decision provided the perfect opportunity for Merck to make that argument before the highest patent court. Merck faced one major hurdle: Chief Judge Howard Markey of that court had written an opinion in an earlier case (*FMC Corp. v Manitowoc*) rejecting a no harm, no foul rule. He had held that information deliberately withheld from a patent examiner did not have to make the patent invalid; it only needed to be sufficiently material enough that it might have caused a reasonable patent examiner to deny the patent. Judge

Schwartz relied on the *FMC* precedent to declare the Flexeril patent unenforceable.

My brief on the appeal was short and made only two points. First, whether the withheld information would have been material to the patent examiner is a question of fact on which a trial court judge cannot be overruled unless the decision was "clearly erroneous." Appeal courts rarely substitute their judgment for the trial judge's judgment on questions of fact, especially when the trial judge is a distinguished jurist like Judge Schwartz, who always crafted thorough opinions. Second, it was clear that Judge Schwartz had correctly applied the law established by Chief Judge Markey in the *FMC* case.

The oral argument on the Flexeril case occurred in the winter of 1989. Fortunately for me, Chief Judge Markey was the presiding judge. I was home free! Each side had thirty minutes to present an oral argument. I did not need to waste time explaining the law. When my turn came, I made a bold move. I summarized Judge Schwartz's opinion in less than five minutes to confirm its thoroughness and establish that the appeals court had no basis for substituting its judgment on the facts. Then I looked directly at Judge Markey and said, "Your Honor, Judge Schwartz's finding that Merck made material misrepresentations is a fact that cannot be reversed unless it is clearly erroneous. It is not. He specifically relied on your opinion in *FMC* to conclude that the information withheld by Merck only had to be of sufficient importance that it could have caused the examiner to deny the patent. Therefore, you only have two choices. You can affirm Judge Schwartz's decision or reverse your decision in *FMC*. If there are no questions, I will reserve the balance of my time." I sat down.

You could feel the shock and disbelief in the gallery of lawyers watching the argument. I had ended my presentation even though I had twenty minutes left. That seldom happens. Lawyers usually keep talking until their time is up. It was pointless to speak that long when the issue was clear-cut. I didn't want to risk getting dragged into an argument about the evidence supporting Judge Schwartz's decision. Joe Fitzpatrick was stuck in a difficult situation. He could only win by either attacking Judge Schwartz on the facts or the Chief Judge on the law. He tried to do both. It did not go well for him.

In early May 1989, the Federal Circuit Court of Appeals affirmed Judge Schwartz (*Merck v Danbury*, 873 F.2d 1418 (Fed. Cir. 1989)). Danbury was free to launch the first generic version of Flexeril and would do so by the beginning of the summer. When I received the news, I was alone in a hotel room in Oklahoma City, where I was preparing my cardiology expert to testify at the Ciba-Geigy beta-blocker trial. I couldn't hold back the tears thinking about how much I missed Jane and how proud she would have been.

The trial challenging Ciba-Geigy's patent on Lopressor was scheduled to begin in New York the day after Mother's Day. I had been preparing for a beta-blocker trial for four years and was ready. There was still a lot of preparation to get a cardiologist, a medicinal chemist, and a patent lawyer prepared to testify as expert witnesses. The week before the trial, Ciba-Geigy reached out to discuss the possibility of a settlement. I didn't care whether the case was settled or not. I had been preparing for a beta-blocker trial for almost four years and felt confident about the outcome. So, I decided to leave the settlement discussions to Jay Schein and remain focused on preparing for trial. The settlement discussions began on Friday morning, only three days before the trial began. They dragged on for hours. I was sure Jay preferred to go to trial and gamble on a big win. However, a settlement would provide much-needed capital for Schein's recent acquisition of a factory to produce sterile, injectable, generic drugs in Phoenix.

It was mid-afternoon when Jay called to say he had agreed to settle the litigation for a cash payment of $9 million. It was a proud moment for me. The strategy I devised at my kitchen table five years earlier had succeeded. I had battled three of the largest pharmaceutical companies in the world, represented by elite teams of lawyers, and I had beaten them all. They hadn't killed me as Tom Garvey had predicted. David had defeated Goliath.

Danbury began selling cyclobenzaprine in June 1989 at a wholesale price of forty-two cents a pill. The excess profit was thirty-nine cents. Thanks to state generic substitution laws, it was only a matter of weeks before Schein's generic Flexeril filled more than 90 percent of all prescriptions for the drug. Three years passed before other generic versions of Flexeril were approved for sale, and the generic price was dramatically reduced to a few cents a pill. By then, my share of the profits had reached $74 million. My life had been permanently altered.

My research in creating the Flexeril patent challenge made me curious about other Merck patents and commercial products related to amitriptyline and cyclobenzaprine. The tricyclic antidepressants, led by Elavil, had been a popular class of drugs for a long time. One of Merck's other products was nortriptyline, an antidepressant with a chemical structure and pharmacological properties similar to Elavil. I spent some time at the New York Academy of Medicine studying tricyclic antidepressants after Jane died when I needed a reason to get out of the house and keep busy. It didn't take me more than a few hours to learn that Elavil is metabolized in the stomach and becomes nortriptyline. It is well known to medicinal chemists that the pharmacological activity of a drug is sometimes produced by its metabolites rather than by the active ingredient in the pill.

The metabolite of a known drug is not patentable because it is not new. Nortriptyline existed in the body of every patient who ever took amitriptyline, whether anyone knew it or not. It is a routine part of the drug development process to identify the metabolites of a new drug and determine if those metabolites contribute to the pharmacologic activity of a drug. The existence of nortriptyline certainly became known to Merck during the development of Elavil.

Drug companies usually try to get around the inability to patent a metabolite as a new molecule by claiming it as a pharmaceutical composition in the form of a tablet or capsule. That composition is technically "new" because the metabolite never existed as a freestanding pill. It should still not be possible to get a valid patent on a metabolite because it would be obvious to use an active metabolite as the active ingredient of a drug instead of another compound from which the metabolite is automatically formed when swallowed. When I first read Merck's nortriptyline patent, I expected to see pharmaceutical composition claims. To my surprise, there were none. Merck had only claimed nortriptyline as a new molecule. The patent was invalid as a matter of law.

By early 1990, Danbury had filed for FDA approval of a generic version of nortriptyline. There was a problem. The nortriptyline patent was going to expire in about three years. Hatch-Waxman prohibited the FDA from approving Danbury's generic application for thirty months unless I could get a court to declare the patent invalid before then. I was confident I could get a district court to declare the nortriptyline patent invalid without a trial. Unfortunately, that would probably take a year, and an appeal would add at least another year. Danbury would be lucky if it could begin marketing a generic version of nortriptyline more than six months before Merck's patent expired, assuming the FDA approved its application by then.

Merck sued Danbury in Delaware federal court and, once again, hired Fitzpatrick, Cella, and Harper & Scinto. Shortly after the litigation began, I proposed a settlement. Danbury would drop the patent challenge in exchange for a license to sell a generic version of nortriptyline that would begin six months before the nortriptyline patent expired. Merck immediately accepted the offer.

They knew their patent would not survive and were not anxious to suffer another embarrassing loss so soon after the Flexeril case. It was also a great deal for Schein since it assured Schein of getting the same head start in the market that, in the best case, it would have gotten through litigation. It was our fourth successful patent challenge in less than four years. Danbury entered the market six months early and produced over $30 million in excess profits before the patent expired.

In June 1989, Danbury finally applied for FDA approval to market a generic version of the beta-blocker Tenormin. This time, there was no settlement. The case went to trial in 1991 before Judge Caleb Wright, an experienced patent trial judge in the Delaware federal district court. I had prepared for a beta-blocker trial twice before settling with Squibb and Ciba-Geigy and was glad to finally get a chance to present my case to a court.

Imperial Chemical Industries (ICI) owned the patent on atenolol (Tenormin). On the first day of the trial, a dozen lawyers were in two rows at ICI's counsel table. ICI's in-house counsel approached my table, where I was sitting alone, and arrogantly asked, "How are you possibly going to try this case against all these lawyers?"

I smiled and said, "I must admit to a small advantage. I don't have to read the Post-it notes."

"I don't understand," he said.

I replied, "I have been preparing this case for six years and know every detail. None of your people are that prepared. They must depend on the Post-it notes everyone will pass back and forth."

My point hit home on the second day of the trial. It was hard to tell which lawyer was in charge on ICI's side. A stream of young lawyers handled different parts of the cross-examinations of my expert witnesses in the early stages of the case. It was confusing and ineffective. When ICI's lead counsel rose for the first time to object, Judge Wright peered down from the bench and asked, "Who are you?" It was an embarrassment.

Toward the end of the trial, the depth of my trial preparation paid an enormous dividend. ICI's cardiology expert gave testimony contradicted by a paper he had published years earlier. I thought there was a chance that might happen, so I had a copy of the publication tucked away in my briefcase. ICI's lawyers strenuously objected when I sought to cross-examine their expert about the publication, claiming I had failed to identify it as an exhibit in pretrial proceedings. I convinced the judge that the document was relevant to the witness's credibility because it contradicted his testimony. He allowed me to use the publication to demolish the witness's credibility.

Judge Wright issued a long and detailed opinion (*ICI v. Danbury*, 777 F. Supp. 330 (D. Del. 1991)) declaring the Tenormin patent invalid. He concluded that: "In light of the explicit teachings of the prior art as to the functional, structural, and utility aspects of the beta-blocker class of compounds, the structural similarities between atenolol and the prior art, the suggestions in the prior art as to techniques to make the modifications necessary to obtain atenolol, atenolol's lack of unexpected properties and advantages over the prior art beta-blockers in the treatment of hypertension…the invention…would have been obvious to one of ordinary skill in the art when the invention was made…."

The decision was an elaborate version of the ten-page memo I had written about the beta-blockers in 1985. The Federal Circuit praised Judge Wright's thoroughness in affirming his decision. By the time the Tenormin patent was declared invalid, it had almost expired. Schein got a minimal head start in the market, and the excess profits were less than the settlements in the prior beta-blocker cases. Nevertheless, it was a priceless personal victory to have the courts agree with the conclusions that had led to giving up my law practice to pursue the patent challenge venture.

I completed two other patent challenges before my first retirement from the patent challenge business in 1995. Each began with a rumor that something was wrong with a patent on an important commercial drug. Danbury personnel often heard such rumors from the suppliers of active pharmaceutical ingredients. The first challenge was a Bristol Myers patent claiming the use of buspirone (Buspar) to treat anxiety. It was yet another case like Flexeril where the compound itself was known, but a patent had been granted for an alleged new medical use. The Buspar patent acknowledged that buspirone had previously been disclosed as a tranquilizer but claimed that using the compound to treat anxiety was a patentable new medical use.

I was dumbfounded when I first read the Buspar patent. My lay understanding was that tranquilizers were commonly used to treat anxiety. *Merriam-Webster*'s *Dictionary* confirmed that a tranquilizer is a drug that treats anxiety or has a calming effect. Every scientific publication I could find confirmed that definition. Along the way, I learned that a class of drugs known as "major tranquilizers" was primarily used to treat more serious mental disorders like depression or schizophrenia. These major tranquilizers were also known to have a calming effect. Using buspirone to treat anxiety wasn't new and could not be the subject of a valid patent. All any judge had to do was give the word tranquilizer its ordinary meaning to reach that conclusion.

Danbury filed an Abbreviated New Drug Application seeking FDA approval to market a generic version of buspirone in late 1992. Bristol Myers sued Danbury for patent infringement in the Southern District of New York. I immediately filed a summary judgment motion asking that the patent be declared invalid as a matter of law. In a bold move, I offered no evidence other than the patent itself and argued that the judge only needed to read the patent to understand why that was true. The patent admitted that using buspirone to treat anxiety was not new because it acknowledged that buspirone was a known tranquilizer. It wasn't the first time I had sought to have a patent declared invalid with no evidence other than the patent itself, so I knew it was possible to win. Years earlier, I had successfully invalidated a patent claiming a pre-cut, pre-styled wig produced by giving a wig a haircut and then creating an algorithm to mass-produce duplicates of that haircut by pulling apart the wig and measuring the length and curl of each tufted segment. In that case, I convinced the judge that the patent claimed nothing more than giving a wig a haircut, which was certainly not a new product.

I got the same result in the buspirone case. The district court judge found (*Bristol-Myers Squibb Co. v. Danbury Pharmacal, Inc.*, 825 F. Supp. 58, 28 USPQ2d 1947 (S.D.N.Y. 1993)) that the ordinary meaning of the term "tranquilizer" included drugs that treated anxiety or had a calming effect. Bristol appealed to the Federal Circuit. It argued that the common understanding of "tranquilizer" did not include drugs that treat anxiety. The Federal Circuit reversed the trial court (*Bristol-Myers Squibb Company v. Danbury Pharmacal, Inc.*, 26 F.3d 138 (Fed. Cir. 1994)) and held that the meaning of "tranquilizer" to those skilled in the field was an issue of fact on which Bristol was entitled to present expert testimony at a trial. It was a ridiculous decision because Bristol had not produced convincing evidence of any dispute among experts about the meaning of "tranquilizer," and the trial judge had found that none existed. The trial would be a waste of time, but it would delay generic competition for years. That was worth hundreds of millions of dollars to Bristol.

I went about the tedious task of collecting evidence and deposing Bristol's scientists to prove that everyone understood "tranquilizer" meant drugs that reduce anxiety. Bristol's lawyers used every obnoxious trick in the books to drag out pretrial discovery and delay the trial. Nevertheless, it was clear that Bristol had no case, and the patent would be declared invalid again.

A few weeks before the trial, I received a call from Alan Fox, the Washington lawyer who represented Bristol during the final negotiations leading to the Hatch-Waxman Act. He was calling to explore the possibility of a settlement. I knew there had been some settlement conversations between Schein and Bristol executives about a cash payment of $25 million, but Schein was not interested. Its success in selling a generic version of Flexeril had changed the stakes. Schein felt it could earn $100 million by winning the Buspar patent challenge and launching a generic version. I explained that to Fox and told him that a settlement was unlikely. A few days later, Bristol offered to pay Schein $72 million to withdraw its patent challenge. I was stunned!

Why would Bristol pay such a staggering amount? That was simple. Buspar had $240 million in sales in 1994. The cost of producing the pills was no more than 2 percent of the selling price, leaving Bristol with an annual gross profit of about $235 billion. That profit would disappear within a month or two if Schein launched a generic version of buspirone. If Schein withdrew its patent challenge, there would be no possibility of another generic competitor for thirty months after a new patent challenge was filed. That would produce at least $600 million in additional gross profits for Bristol. Seventy-two million dollars was a small price to pay.

Although Schein could earn $100 million or more in excess profits, it still had to win the lawsuit, survive an appeal, and get FDA approval to sell its generic version of Buspar. It would take a couple of years, and there is always some uncertainty. Any reasonable risk analysis made the proper choice to accept a cash payment of $72 million. Nevertheless, I was concerned that the settlement might violate antitrust laws. It is unlawful for a company to pay a competitor not to compete. Yet a patent gives the owner a legal right to prevent competition. By accepting the settlement, Schein would simply be confirming the status quo created by the patent. It has no obligation to the public to eliminate the patent. Other generic manufacturers would be free to challenge the patent and rely on the same arguments Schein presented. Those arguments were a matter of public record.

Richard Goldberg and his team of antitrust lawyers concluded that Schein's antitrust risks were minimal, and the settlement offer was accepted. I was right to be worried. Years later, whether the payment to Schein was lawful or violated the antitrust laws became the subject of a Federal Trade Commission investigation and, eventually, a Supreme Court decision. The legality of such payments remains a subject of controversy.

My last Schein patent challenge began in 1994. It involved a patent claiming a salt form of vecuronium bromide (Norcuron), an injectable skeletal muscle relaxant used in surgery as an adjunct to anesthesia. An earlier patent claiming vecuronium bromide had expired. The salt form of vecuronium bromide did not change the efficacy or safety of the original drug. It was a more stable form of the original drug, which gave it a longer shelf life.

It was common practice in the pharmaceutical industry to reformulate a new drug into its most stable form once approved. Many drugs before vecuronium bromide had been converted to a more stable salt or hydrate. Standard drug formulation textbooks disclosed the idea of making this change. It was a matter of routine skill in commercializing a drug. There was nothing patentable about it. Unfortunately, the Patent Office routinely grants these patents because patent examiners lack basic knowledge about the level of skill the average worker possesses in the fields they examine. Courts typically find these patents invalid.

I was confident that the patent challenge would be successful, but I didn't need or want the stress of handling another trial alone. I hired my old friends Bill Mentlik and Joe Littenberg of Lerner David in Westfield, New Jersey, to work on the vecuronium case with me for a percentage of my interest. I postponed the contingency arrangement for a few months because I had a hunch that the case might be settled quickly.

The lawsuit was pending in the Arizona federal district court. Although it had just begun, there were already five disputes regarding pretrial discovery. The patent owner was engaged in the harassment and delay tactics that had become the norm in my patent challenge cases. I flew to Phoenix for a hearing on the discovery motions. Before the hearing began, I asked our local Phoenix lawyer if there was any possibility we could get the judge to set a trial date. He said the judge had a reputation for letting cases drag on and would not give us a trial date.

When it was my turn to present an argument, I decided to gamble. I told the judge that all the motions on both sides were bullshit—although I did not use that word—and could easily be compromised by the lawyers without wasting the court's time. I also said we would be back every few weeks with more petty fights because my opponents were hellbent on doing everything possible to delay a trial. "Your Honor," I concluded, "there's one way to stop all this discovery nonsense. If you give us an early trial date now, the case will likely be settled, and you will never see us again." My chutzpah flabbergasted the local lawyers but didn't bother the judge. A few days later, he set a trial date. Shortly after that, we agreed on a settlement.

Like the nortriptyline settlement, the vecuronium settlement granted Schein a license to begin selling a competing generic product six months before the patent expiration date. But the license agreement set a specific starting date and did not mention the patent expiration date. Sometime after the agreement was signed, the patent law was changed so that patents expired twenty years after they were first filed rather than seventeen years after they were granted. The expiration date of the vecuronium patent was extended by nineteen months, and the Schein license began twenty-five months before the patent expired.

In 1994, Schein decided to go public. The effort failed because Wall Street bankers recognized that most of Schein's profits mostly came from litigation revenue, and future earnings were uncertain. Schein eventually sold a 25 percent stake in its generic drug business to Bayer for $300 million. In just ten years, Schein's market value had risen from about $10 million to $1.2 billion.

You had to be the first challenger to profit from patent challenges. The 180-day Hatch-Waxman market exclusivity awarded to the first challenger was critical. Being first was never an issue during the ten years of my Schein venture because no other generic drug manufacturers were actively engaged in challenging patents. I only recall one challenge filed by Biocraft Laboratories involving Moduretic, a potassium-sparing diuretic drug.

The publicity surrounding Schein's financial success sparked the interest of every generic manufacturer. They were all lawyering up and looking for patent challenges. It was likely that multiple generic manufacturers would challenge the same patents, and the timing of challenges would become critical. That would dramatically increase the risk that the Schein venture would continue to be successful. I had already made a fortune and was burned out. There was no reason for me to continue. It was time for me to find a new set of challenges that would be less stressful and allow me to enjoy the fruits of what I had accomplished. I stopped practicing law and started devoting my time to philanthropy, public policy, and enjoying life.

Unfortunately, Schein decided to pursue one of my suggested patent challenges on their own. The challenge involved Pepcid, a member of a class of H2 receptor blockers useful for treating ulcers. Pepcid was a me-too drug discovered after Zantac, and the basis for the patent challenge was analogous to the beta-blocker cases. All H2 blockers discovered after Zantac had a common molecular structure and produced comparable clinical outcomes despite minor differences in chemical structure. Unfortunately, Schein's new lawyers made several strategic errors, including producing a privileged memo I had written early in the project's development that included a technical error regarding differences in the chemical structure of some members of the class. That problem was compounded when Bernie Love, the medicinal chemistry expert who had done a fantastic job in the beta-blocker cases, gave testimony during a pretrial deposition that was highly damaging to the case. I urged Schein to give up its patent challenge and dismiss the case before trial. I felt certain Schein would lose and the court might find the challenge frivolous and require Schein to pay the patent owner's legal fees. My advice was ignored, but it was accurate. The decision (*Yamanuchi et al. v. Danbury*, 21 F. Supp 2nd 366 (SDNY 1998)) was critical of my role in recommending the patent challenge. It was a blemish on my perfect record of success in patent challenges. Nobody is perfect.

Almost a decade later, a casual dinner conversation with Phil Frost rekindled my interest in patent challenges. Phil was the CEO of Ivax, a major generic drug manufacturer. He suggested I come out of retirement and work part-time, providing oversight and guidance to Ivax's patent challenge efforts. I was intrigued by the idea but doubted we could ever negotiate a suitable agreement. Phil had previously expressed the belief that Schein drastically overpaid me even though I had created and successfully executed the patent challenges. Everyone else in the industry wished I had partnered with them.

The discussion with Phil made me wonder whether I still had the skills needed to find patents that were worth challenging. By then, everyone in the generic drug business was searching for them. The world had changed dramatically in the twenty years since I studied the beta-blockers at the New York Academy of Medicine. Everything was on the internet now. Copies of patents, patent application files, FDA records, medical journals, and drug sales information were all only a few mouse clicks away. It might be fun to see if I could use the internet to find new patent challenges.

Within a few hours, I had a list of all drugs with annual sales of $100 million or more and patents with more than five years of remaining life. There were about forty drugs on that list. In a few more hours, I had skimmed through the patent claims and eliminated every drug that had a patent claiming the drug molecule. Despite my success with the beta-blockers, patents claiming the new drug molecule, even if they were me-too drugs in the same class, were the least susceptible to a successful patent challenge because the Federal Circuit had become a highly pro-patent court. I was left with ten drugs where the drug molecule was not new and the drug was only protected by a patent claiming a formulation, a new use, or some other feature. It only took a few days to review the proceedings leading to the grant of the ten patents to understand why the patent examiner had granted them. After that, I did some research to see if published information was available that either undermined the patent examiner's rationale for granting the patent or proved that the arguments made by the patent applicant to grant the patent were false. In just fifty or sixty hours of effort, I had identified four worthwhile patent challenges covering commercially important drugs. It was amazing how easy it was to gather the facts and documents online.

I never made a deal with Phil Frost, and I spent more than a year looking for a manufacturing partner for each potential patent challenge. It was far more difficult than I had imagined. The family-owned businesses that formed GPIA had all been sold to big companies for large sums. These companies had their own patent challenge programs and did not want partners. Others were unwilling to make a profit-sharing deal. As time passed, three of the four challenges I had identified were no longer viable because someone else had already begun a challenge or it was too late to bring it because the patent was approaching its expiration date.

My last possible challenge involved an eye drop for treating glaucoma sold by Merck under the brand name Cosopt. Cosopt was a combination of two known drugs that had been individually used to treat glaucoma and were no longer protected by patents. The law was clear: combining two drugs known to be useful for the same purpose was not patentable. There was a narrow exception for situations that produced a highly unexpected result. One plus one had to equal three or more. Merck claimed that was the case with Cosopt. But it wasn't true. The FDA had explicitly rejected Merck's claim that the combination of timolol and dorzolamide produced a superior result. Yet Merck presented the same superiority argument to the patent examiner while failing to mention that the experts at the FDA had already rejected it.

I eventually found Hi-Tech Pharmacal, a small family-owned generic manufacturer on Long Island that could manufacture eye drops. They were thrilled to have the opportunity to work with me under the same terms as the Schein agreement. Hi-Tech prepared an application seeking approval for a generic version of Cosopt, and I prepared a formal patent challenge document. To my surprise, within days after the challenge was filed, Merck disclaimed two of the three patents. It was the third time in my career that I had challenged Merck for fraudulently procuring a patent. This time, the evidence was so compelling that they wisely decided to give up without a fight.

Merck's third patent raised a technical legal question about whether it was eligible for a patent extension under Hatch-Waxman. I hired Bill Mentlik to argue the case before the Federal Circuit. We lost. I vividly remember the oral argument before the Federal Circuit Court of Appeals. Bill was at the podium presenting our argument. I was stretched out on a bench in the courtroom's back row, writhing in pain from trying to pass a kidney stone. At times,

I couldn't tell whether the pain I was experiencing was from the kidney stone or my anguish over not having presented the argument myself.

Old soldiers never die. We always believe our advocacy skills are the difference between winning and losing. The truth is that engaging in courtroom advocacy is not very different from playing professional sports. There is no place for those who have passed their prime. Curled up on that bench, I realized my retirement from litigation was permanent.

Despite the adverse Federal Court decision, Hi-Tech's successful challenge to the two disclaimed Merck patents gave Hi-Tech a head start in launching the first generic version of Cosopt. Its earnings soared, and its publicly traded stock increased sevenfold within a few months. The family sold the business and made a fortune. Knowing I had not lost my talent for creating successful patent challenges was gratifying. But I was about to celebrate my 70th birthday and had no desire to do another.

Everything I learned about patent law from my first day as a patent examiner in 1961 taught me that the system for granting patents in the United States was deeply flawed. My success in the Schein venture was based on a deep understanding of those flaws and the ability to educate judges on how applicants game the patent system to procure invalid patents. When I look back at the patents I successfully challenged, I realize that none would have existed had the patent applicant honestly disclosed what was already known or if the patent examiner knew more about the subject matter. Our patent system is broken and does not operate in the public interest. It does not "...promote the [p]rogress of [s]cience and useful [a]rts..." as the Constitution intended. Instead, it creates an incentive to wrongfully eliminate competition by procuring and enforcing patents of little merit.

Chapter Eight

BRAND/GENERIC ISSUES AFTER HATCH-WAXMAN

I CONTINUED TO REPRESENT THE Generic Pharmaceutical Industry Association (GPIA) after leaving my law firm in 1985. It was important because we expected PhRMA to do whatever was possible to undermine Hatch-Waxman and hinder generic competition. It didn't take long for our expectations to be fulfilled.

Before 1988, a patent claiming a manufacturing process could only be infringed if the manufacturing occurred in the United States. Importing a product manufactured abroad by a process claimed in a US patent was not patent infringement. In 1987, PhRMA supported legislation aimed at changing that law. It was potentially catastrophic for generic drug manufacturers since the active ingredient of most generic drugs is manufactured abroad. Brand-name drug manufacturers owned thousands of US patents claiming methods for manufacturing active pharmaceutical ingredients. Generic manufacturers would have no way to determine if the products they were purchasing were made using an infringing process. The manufacturing methods used by foreign manufacturers were trade secrets they did not disclose to customers. If patent infringement claims were asserted against them, they would be defenseless.

There are usually several commercially viable ways to make the active ingredient of a drug. If the patented methods are disclosed, finding an unpatented method is easy. GPIA dispatched me to Capitol Hill to educate legislators about the basic unfairness of the legislation. I argued that the bill should require brand-name manufacturers to identify all manufacturing patents that might be infringed, just as Hatch-Waxman required them to identify product patents that might be violated. That would make it easy to avoid infringement and get indemnification against infringement claims from foreign suppliers. Brand-name drug manufacturers and patent bar associations vigorously opposed my proposal. They wanted process patent infringement to be a "gotcha" game that would entrap importers and make it difficult for them to compete.

In 1988, I testified before the Subcommittee on Patents at a hearing chaired by Sen. Dennis DeConcini (D-AZ) and explained the problem. DeConcini was sympathetic. He asked the American Patent Law Association chair, who was testifying on the same panel, why it wouldn't be fair to require patent owners to identify their process patents so inadvertent patent infringement could be avoided. To everyone's surprise, he answered that large companies owned so many patents covering manufacturing processes that it would be difficult for them to determine which patents might be infringed. DeConcini exploded. "If you can't identify the relevant patents, how can you reasonably expect the importers of products to do so!"

I drafted an amendment to the proposed legislation that enabled a generic manufacturer to request the maker of a branded drug to identify all relevant process patents. If a patent was not identified, a claim that the patent had been infringed could not be asserted. The law was enacted in that form. It has minimized the use of manufacturing patents to block generic competition.

In 1993, shortly after the inauguration of Bill Clinton, rumors were circulating that Bob Armitage, Eli Lilly's chief patent counsel, was a leading contender to be Under Secretary of

Commerce for Economic Affairs and director of the US Patent and Trademark Office. The generic drug industry feared that, if appointed, Armitage would make it easier for brand-name drug manufacturers to procure meritless secondary patents to delay competition from generic drugs after the basic patent on a new drug expired. While I was out of the country on vacation, and without my knowledge or consent, GPIA proposed to the Clinton administration that I receive the appointment rather than Armitage. I only learned of it when I was invited for a personal interview with Secretary of Commerce Ron Brown.

The Patent Office was a mess. Any effort to reform it would be a serious challenge. It was not the right time in my life. I married Gail May in 1990 after my first wife's passing and was building a new life. I also feared that continuing to receive revenue from prior successful patent challenges might create the appearance of a conflict of interest. That could cost me millions in lost income. Despite my misgivings, I decided to attend the interview and was leaning toward accepting the position if offered.

As I walked down the halls of the Department of Commerce on my way to the Secretary's office for the interview, I had a bit of an anxiety attack. The memories of being in that building working as a patent examiner thirty years earlier flooded my mind. "Oh my God," I thought, "What am I doing here? Nobody can fix all the things that are wrong with this place."

Moments later, I settled into a chair in front of Secretary Brown. His first question was, "Why would somebody as successful as you even consider taking this job?"

Without hesitation, I said: "I never served in the military and felt obligated to serve my country if asked. I also have the ego to believe I can make a difference." We had a cordial discussion.

Secretary Brown asked me what I would do to improve the operation of the Patent Office. I told him I would fire most of the lawyers and hire librarians. "Why?" he asked.

I said, "Because you can't make good decisions about granting patents without all the relevant facts. Patent examiners don't have the skills or resources to determine whether a patent application is sufficiently different from what is already known to justify the grant of a patent."

I heard nothing for several weeks after the interview and began to worry that I was still in the running. Finally, one afternoon, I returned home and saw the flashing light on the answering machine. A voice on the phone said that Secretary Brown wanted to thank me for my willingness to be considered, but the White House was announcing the appointment of Bruce Lehman as the new director of the Patent Office. I felt like I had won the Powerball lottery. And it was certainly good news for the generic drug industry that PhRMA's pick was not appointed. In retrospect, I can't help wondering whether I missed an opportunity to implement policies that might have reduced the number of invalid pharmaceutical patents granted by the Patent Office.

As a consolation prize, I was appointed to IFAC-3, one of several advisory committees created by the Clinton administration to give the private sector direct input into trade policy issues. IFAC-3 was devoted to the global enforcement of intellectual property rights under the Agreement on Trade-Related Aspects of Intellectual Property Rights (TRIPS), which came into force in 1995. It was packed with lobbyists and lawyers for the pharmaceutical, movie, recording, and computer software industries. Their job was to convince the US government to impose strict intellectual property enforcement against developing nations to protect the monopoly profits of their clients globally.

By the time I took my seat on IFAC-3, my role as counsel to the GPIA had ended. In 1994, when Schein first explored the possibility of becoming a public company, every generic drug manufacturer became aware of the enormous sums we had earned from the patent challenge venture. They were all eager to enter the patent challenge business. When one jealous member of the GPIA board suggested that my legal advice to the trade association might be tainted by my interest in the Schein patent challenge venture, I immediately resigned as GPIA's counsel. That put me in the unusual position of being the only member of the IFAC-3 who was not formally representing the interests of a client or industry.

The PhRMA lobbyists on IFAC-3 were pushing the US Trade Representative, Mickey Kantor, for global enforcement of pharmaceutical patents that went far beyond the requirements of US law. In some cases, they were inconsistent with Hatch-Waxman. As one example, PhRMA wanted the Trade Representative to ignore the *Bolar* exemption and require other nations to prohibit generic manufacturers from developing competitive generic drugs until after all patents expired. The Office of the Trade Representative was not familiar with the *Bolar* exemption and the other special patent provisions of Hatch-Waxman. I educated them. Eventually, they rejected all efforts to impose patent enforcement requirements on developing countries that were more stringent than US law.

Drug companies were also wrongfully claiming that the five-year Hatch-Waxman exclusivity for unpatented new drugs was based on an exclusive property right in the clinical data submitted to get a new drug approved. It wasn't true; The Hatch-Waxman Act and its legislative history do not mention or recognize any property rights in clinical data. The Congressional floor debate over the five-year exclusivity described it as a market exclusivity intended to provide a minimum level of protection for new drugs that were not patentable. In truth, the exclusivity provision was a last-minute "bone" we had thrown to the dissident PhRMA manufacturers to drop their opposition to the enactment of Hatch-Waxman. "Data exclusivity" was a concept fabricated by PhRMA after the passage of Hatch-Waxman to bully other countries into creating a new monopoly right that would last longer than five years and would provide a monopoly for every approved new drug independent of the existence or validity of patents.

The South Centre, an organization based in Argentina, was a leading voice in opposing efforts by developed nations to use intellectual property rights to hinder economic growth in developing nations. I wrote a paper published as an appendix to a South Centre publication arguing against the claim that Hatch-Waxman had created a new property right in clinical data. In it, I explained the origins of Hatch-Waxman's five-year market exclusivity and proposed that foreign countries adopt a five-year market exclusivity that began and ended when the US market exclusivity began and ended.

At that time, I was also the chair of the Myers-JDC-Brookdale Institute, a nonprofit applied social research think tank in Israel, which was a joint venture between the government of Israel and the American Jewish Joint Distribution Committee. That position brought me into contact with many senior government officials in Israel. They enlisted my help in dealing with a threat by the US Trade Representative to impose trade sanctions against Israel for failing to adopt a five-year exclusivity law for new drugs. I urged Israel to enact a law granting a five-year market exclusivity for new drugs, which ran from the date a new drug was first approved in the United States rather than Israel. They did so. PhRMA was outraged and demanded the imposition of sanctions. They wanted the five-year exclusivity to run from the date a new drug was registered for sale in Israel. The controversy got the attention of Senator Chuck Schumer (D-NY), a staunch supporter of Israel.

Once I explained the situation, he pressured the Trade Representative to back off. Despite my limited success, PhRMA continued to press for "data exclusivity" worldwide, and its efforts met little resistance. Monopolies of up to ten years based on data exclusivity, market exclusivity, or other theories that did not require the existence of a patent were adopted in the European Union, Japan, and other markets. Twenty-five years later, when the biologic counterpart to Hatch-Waxman, known as the Biologic Price Competition and Innovation Act (BPCIA), was enacted as part of the Affordable Care Act, colloquially known as Obamacare, the pharmaceutical and biotech industries were able to rely on the existence of data protection laws abroad to convince Congress to grant twelve years of exclusivity to every new biologic even if there were no patents claiming the new drug. The enactment of the BPCIA by Congress paved the way for today's drug price crisis.

After a few years, I resigned from IFAC-3. Most of IFAC-3's agenda related to topics of interest to the movie, recording, and software industries, and attending the regular meetings in Washington was a waste of my time. By then, I had established a relationship with the Trade Representative officials responsible for enforcing pharmaceutical intellectual property, and we continued to stay in touch as issues arose. The time I spent as a member of IFAC-3 gave me the confidence to believe I could play a useful role as an independent, pro bono advocate for affordable medicines. I have been doing so ever since.

By the late 1990s, more than a decade after the enactment of Hatch-Waxman, the share of prescriptions filled with a generic drug had doubled (from 19 to 43 percent), and consumers saved over $10 billion. Unquestionably, the abbreviated approval process for generic drugs enacted as part of Hatch-Waxman had succeeded in making low-cost generic drugs much more available. Yet, during the same period, brand-name drug sales soared from $20 billion to $250 billion, largely due to the introduction of blockbuster drugs such as Tenormin, Lipitor, Zantac, Nexium, and dozens more for treating chronic conditions like hypertension, high cholesterol, gastric distress, and depression that affected tens of millions of patients. It would have been easy to conclude that Hatch-Waxman had also achieved its goal of creating an incentive to invest in discovering new drugs. However, there was no evidence that the patent term extensions created by Hatch-Waxman had been the driving force behind the investment in discovering new drugs. It was simply happenstance that the enactment of Hatch-Waxman coincided with a golden era in new drug discoveries.

I decided the time was ripe for me to write a law review article that would provide historians with a history of how the key provisions of Hatch-Waxman were born and an analysis of whether they were accomplishing their intended purpose. "Special Patent Provisions for Pharmaceuticals: Have They Outlived Their Usefulness?" was published in 1999. In it, I expressed the opinion that all the extra monopoly protections enacted by Hatch-Waxman were not serving any useful purpose and should be repealed. My article has been cited hundreds of times and has been the usual starting point for the numerous scholarly critiques of Hatch-Waxman over the last twenty-five years.

The Bolar exemption in Hatch-Waxman, which authorized the FDA to tentatively approve competitive generic drugs early so that competition could begin on the day the basic patent claiming a new drug expired, had effectively nullified the patent term extensions granted by Hatch-Waxman. The average patent term extensions granted under Hatch-Waxman had increased the amount of patent life remaining on the date the FDA approved a new drug by two to three years. But the Bolar exemption eliminated two to three years of monopoly that brand-name drugs would have enjoyed after a patent expired. Drug manufacturers were making record profits even though the length of basic patent protection for a new drug was unchanged. I had vigorously argued before Hatch-Waxman was enacted that patent extensions were unnecessary. Time proved that my assessment was correct.

And I was proud that my role in creating the Bolar exemption had produced that result.

On the other hand, the patent certification provisions of Hatch-Waxman, which I envisioned as a pathway for accelerating generic competition by flushing out invalid patents, were being gamed by brand-name drug manufacturers to make billions in unjustified extra monopoly profits. Brand-name manufacturers acquired many secondary patents on every commercially important drug to delay legitimate generic competition. These patents claimed routine drug formulation techniques such as changes to inactive ingredients, the dosage form, or the form of the active ingredient, which did not affect the safety or efficacy of the new drug. When challenged, courts routinely ruled that these patents were invalid and should never have been granted by the Patent Office. Nevertheless, listing a meritless secondary patent with the FDA and claiming it would be infringed if a generic drug was approved triggered an automatic thirty-month delay in approving the competitive generic product.

Brand-name manufacturers quickly recognized they could delay generic competition even longer than thirty months by paying a generic challenger to drop a patent challenge against a meritless secondary patent. That is precisely what happened in my Bristol Myers BusPar patent challenge. Bristol's $72 million payment to Schein ended the litigation. It allowed Bristol to earn hundreds of millions in additional monopoly profits for several years since no other generic challenger to the BusPar patent emerged. I didn't believe Schein violated the antitrust laws in accepting the payment because Bristol's monopoly resulted from the existence of the patent and not from Schein's agreement to forego a challenge to the patent. No law required Schein to pursue a costly patent challenge with an uncertain outcome. But it was far less clear to me that, rather than enforcing its patent, the patent owner could pay off potential patent challengers so they would refrain from seeking to compete. By the time I published my article, these so-called reverse payments had become common and were under investigation by the Federal Trade Commission and State Attorney Generals.

The automatic thirty-month delay in approving a generic drug whenever a patent was asserted was intended to protect brand-name manufacturers from willful infringement of the basic patent claiming a new drug. No one involved in drafting Hatch-Waxman contemplated the possibility that patents claiming changes to an approved drug could block FDA approval of a generic drug for thirty months. My law review article called for repealing or modifying the thirty-month rule so that could not happen.

Some executives of the generic drug industry were infuriated by my article. One told me: "Now that you have gotten rich from the law you wrote, you want to deny the same opportunity to others in the industry." Nothing could have been further from the truth. The patent certification provisions were created to prevent bad patents from blocking generic competition and not to promote lucrative settlements between brand and generic manufacturers. It never occurred to me that brand-name manufacturers would pay generic challenges large sums to avoid having their patents adjudicated. Most generic manufacturers did not even engage in patent challenges during the decade after Hatch-Waxman was first enacted. They only began to think about the possibility after they became aware that payments were being made in some cases and patents were being declared invalid in others. I was convinced that it was not in the best interests of the generic drug industry to delay generic competition by expanding the use of reverse payment settlements. Hatch-Waxman was intended to accelerate generic competition, not to delay it.

More than a decade after my article, the US Supreme Court ruled that reverse payments might violate the anti-trust laws.

It held that whether a patent settlement violated anti-trust law must be decided under the rule of reason after examining the terms of each agreement. The law now requires agreements settling drug patent challenges to be submitted to the FTC for review. Legislation to outlaw such settlements is pending before Congress but has stalled.

Chapter Nine

GOVERNMENT PROCUREMENT OF PRESCRIPTION DRUGS—THE CIPRO CONTROVERSY

My law review article in *IDEA* made me think about other issues that were overlooked in the process of enacting Hatch-Waxman. One error was that the law may have inadvertently made it more difficult for the US government to purchase generic versions of patented drugs for government use. I never would have realized it but for my time as a lawyer at the Justice Department in the 1960s, during which I was involved in the government's procurement of tranquilizer drugs from Scandinavia.

The US government and its suppliers are immune to claims of patent infringement. This creates a potential conflict with the Hatch-Waxman Act because the FDA is prohibited from approving a generic drug unless the generic manufacturer certifies that any patents listed by the brand-name drug owner are invalid or not infringed. Generic drug manufacturers cannot sell drugs to the government unless they are FDA-approved. Therefore, the patent certification provisions of Hatch-Waxman appear to interfere with the government's patent immunity. The issue never arose during the Hatch-Waxman negotiations. It was an oversight. Can a generic manufacturer seeking to sell a generic copy of a patented drug to the government get around the patent certification requirements of Hatch-Waxman? I decided to dig deeper to see if there was an answer.

Legal precedent firmly established that the government's immunity from patent infringement extends to its suppliers and potential suppliers. I found one case where a New Jersey federal district court granted an injunction preventing a generic manufacturer from making future sales of an infringing generic drug but permitted the manufacturer to continue manufacturing and selling the drug to the government. That convinced me there was a simple solution to the Hatch-Waxman patent certification requirement for sales to the government. A generic manufacturer seeking approval to sell generic drugs to the government could certify that "No listed patent will be infringed because the drug will be sold solely to the US government. The government and its suppliers are immune from claims for patent infringement. The patent owner's sole remedy is to sue the United States for reasonable compensation under 28 USC §1498." Simply put, the FDA is compelled to approve generic drugs for sale to the government without regard to patents.

I thought about coming out of retirement to test my theory but decided against it. Instead, I wrote a memo summarizing my legal research and filed it on my computer. I knew a situation would eventually arise to make the memo relevant.

I didn't have to wait long. In October 2001, shortly after the 9/11 terrorist attacks, the country faced a major bioterrorism threat because envelopes containing anthrax were being mailed to public figures. I was attending a monthly breakfast of health policy leaders in New York City when I learned that there was widespread hoarding of Cipro, the only FDA-approved treatment for anthrax, which had created a critical shortage.

Several generic manufacturers had tentative FDA approval to manufacture a generic version of Cipro but were blocked from entering the market because of a challenge to Bayer's Cipro patent by Barr Laboratories. Barr was the first generic manufacturer to challenge the Cipro patent and was entitled to 180 days of market exclusivity before the other tentatively-approved generic manufacturers could launch their products. Barr delayed its product launch while Bayer appealed a trial court judgment declaring the Cipro patent was unenforceable because Bayer had withheld material information from the Patent Examiner.

I was in a taxi headed home after the breakfast meeting when the radio announced that Tom Brokaw had just received an anthrax envelope. I then realized that the memo on my computer concerning the government's patent immunity provided a path to make generic Cipro immediately available for government use. The government could use its patent immunity to authorize the tentatively-approved generic manufacturers to produce Cipro for sale to a government stockpile.

I needed political help to make this happen, so I called Senator Chuck Schumer. Schumer was aware of my expertise on drug patents and understood the political importance of assuring the public that adequate supplies of Cipro would be available to treat anthrax. I told him I could have a formal legal memo in his hands in a couple of hours. I urged him to enlist the help of Agnes Varis, the CEO of Agvar Chemicals Inc., a supplier of active ingredients to generic drug manufacturers, to confirm that the tentatively-approved generic manufacturers were willing and able to produce generic Cipro if they could get FDA approval. Chuck knew and trusted Agnes, who was one of his major donors.

The following day, October 17, 2001, the *New York Times* carried a front-page story stating: "Senator Charles E. Schumer, Democrat of New York, proposed today that the government buy generic versions of Cipro for its emergency stockpile, noting that such a step would reduce dependence on a single supplier and could significantly reduce the costs of getting the amount of ciprofloxacin needed." Over the next week, Chuck and I engaged in discussions with Tommy Thompson, Secretary of Health in the Bush administration, and his counsel, Alex Azar, who would later become health secretary in the Trump Administration. They resisted the idea that US law allowed the government to disregard Bayer's Cipro patent even though they could not find any flaw in my legal memo. Eventually, they used the threat of implementing my proposal to bully Bayer into increasing its production of Cipro, dedicating 50 percent of its output to direct sales to the government to create a stockpile and reducing the price charged to the government by 50 percent to $1.80/pill.

It was a bad business deal for the government but a great political victory. I would have preferred to see my legal strategy implemented to create a stockpile of generic Cipro at a much lower cost. Generic Cipro was available in international markets at five to ten cents a pill compared to the $1.80 the government had agreed to pay Bayer. Nevertheless, I was pleased that my effort established the principle that the US government had patent immunity and might exercise it in an emergency.

The timing of the Cipro controversy could not have been better for developing nations. The Doha round of trade negotiations was scheduled for the following month. Developing countries wanted the right to use compulsory licensing of patents to access lower-cost drugs in national health emergencies. The US Trade Representative, egged on by the pharmaceutical lobby, was opposed. I seized the opportunity to challenge the US position in an interview with the Washington Post on October 20, 2001. They reported: "Alfred Engelberg, a retired intellectual property lawyer who wrote a brief for Schumer about the propriety of the government action, said the Government's reluctance to order generic Cipro stemmed from a larger concern: For years, drugmakers and the U.S. government have clashed with developing countries in Asia and Africa over the right for them to acquire generic medicines for AIDS and other diseases. 'If the U.S. is seen as issuing a compulsory license when it has a health emergency, it can hardly argue to the rest of the world that third-world countries can't exercise a similar right when they have an emergency,' he said."

The US Trade Representative backed down. Three weeks later, with the approval of the United States, the Doha Declaration affirmed the right of developing nations to use compulsory patent licensing to acquire drugs to meet health emergencies. The debate over when, where, and how the exercise of a compulsory license is appropriate continues today. But the principle remains firmly established in international trade law.

A private citizen rarely gets to play a critical role in influencing government action on an important issue. To do so, you must have access to policymakers. The reputation I had developed on Capitol Hill as the lawyer for the generic drug industry had created access for me. Lawmakers and their staff were open to taking my calls and even called me when they needed advice on drug issues. I had carved out a niche as an independent expert on ways to make prescription drugs more accessible and affordable. And I have continued to use that platform over the last few decades.

Unfortunately, getting positive outcomes on policy issues is much harder than winning lawsuits, especially because of the impact of lobbying and campaign contributions by the pharmaceutical and biotech industries. As drug prices have skyrocketed in recent years, many progressive scholars have argued that the government should proactively use its immunity from claims of patent infringement to purchase low-cost generic drugs for government health insurance programs such as Medicare, Medicaid, and military procurement. They often cite the Cipro controversy and my legal memo to Schumer as evidence of the viability of this approach. Yet the concept remains untested. To date, no generic manufacturer has sought FDA approval to bypass the patent certification requirements of Hatch-Waxman for sales to the government. Yet government health insurance programs account for nearly 50 percent of all prescription drug purchases in the United States.

Using the government's patent immunity to avoid infringement of basic patents and drive down the cost of new drugs would be controversial because it could chill investment in discovering new drugs. But the government's patent immunity could still be a powerful weapon to prevent pharmaceutical companies from using meritless secondary patents claiming minor changes to a drug to delay generic competition. This would be especially true in situations involving drugs discovered with federal funding where the government already owns a royalty-free license to practice the basic patent claiming a drug and is free to manufacture a low-cost generic drug for government programs without compensating the patent owner.

Chapter Ten

USING PHILANTHROPY TO ADVANCE PUBLIC POLICY

EARLY IN THE NEW MILLENNIUM, brand-name drug manufacturers began to face a patent cliff as the patents on the first blockbuster drug in each therapeutic class began expiring. "Patent cliff" was the phrase coined by Wall Street to describe the abrupt loss in profits suffered by the brand-name drug manufacturer when a patent expired and low-cost generic versions flooded the market. Generics routinely captured over 90 percent of all prescriptions within a month or two, thanks to mandatory generic substitution under state pharmacy laws.

Blockbuster drugs like Mevacor to treat high cholesterol, Prilosec for gastric reflux, and Prozac to treat depression spurred many me-too imitators with patents that expired later. It was pointless for a brand-name manufacturer to continue marketing a drug after its patents expired because generic substitution laws assured that almost all prescriptions for the brand-name drug would be filled with a lower-cost generic. That marketing void created the opportunity for the manufacturers of me-too drugs that were still protected by patents to increase their sales by aggressive marketing to physicians. Doctors would routinely prescribe a patented member of the drug class to a new patient rather than a lower-cost generic member of the same class because they could give the patient free samples with the initial prescription and get wined and dined by the manufacturer for doing so. The rise in prescriptions for Crestor after the expiration of patents on Lipitor or Nexium after Prilosec became generic was significant. Yet it made no economic sense for patients to take a patented me-too drug rather than the generic version of the original blockbuster. They could save as much as $1000/year by taking a generic drug in the same class and still get the same clinical benefit. Unfortunately, patients lacked the information they needed to know they had that choice.

Several reputable scientific institutions were doing studies to evaluate the comparative clinical effectiveness of drugs that treat the same medical condition. The Veterans Administration used its studies to switch veterans to the lowest-cost, clinically effective medicine. The Drug Effectiveness Review Project (DERP) based at the Oregon Health & Science University Evidence-based Practice Center was providing comparative effectiveness information to many state Medicaid programs. These studies proved that the me-too drugs produced little or no difference in clinical outcomes for most patients. By 2003, Senator Hillary Clinton (D-NY) was spearheading a legislative effort to increase the government's reliance on comparative clinical effectiveness studies to determine which drugs should be dispensed in government health insurance programs. It was likely that PhRMA would block any legislation that sought to undermine the ability of pharmaceutical manufacturers to influence doctors' prescribing habits.

I realized there was a way to educate consumers without waiting for legislation. Consumer Reports was a trusted source of information about the comparative cost and quality of cars, appliances, and other consumer products for millions of consumers. Why couldn't Consumer Reports do for prescription drugs what it was already successfully doing for other products? I decided to ask them. In late 2003, I wrote a letter to Jim Guest, the CEO of Consumers Union and the publisher of Consumer Reports. In it, I introduced myself and described the opportunity to educate consumers about prescription drugs. He was immediately enthusiastic. We scheduled a meeting with his senior staff to discuss the possibility. I offered Consumer Union a $50,000 planning grant from the Engelberg Foundation to develop a program for educating consumers on the comparative effectiveness and cost of drugs that treat the same condition. A decade earlier, I had created and endowed The Engelberg Foundation using some of the millions of dollars I had earned from the successful patent challenges with the intent that the foundation would support worthwhile projects to make healthcare and prescription drugs more affordable.

Within a few months, Consumer Union proposed the creation of user-friendly comparative effectiveness reports that would provide patients with information comparing the effectiveness, safety, side effects, and cost of prescription drugs available to treat the most common chronic conditions. The scientific data would come from DERP. I liked the general idea, but there was a major problem. The proposal was to publish the reports in Consumer Reports magazine, which is only available through a paid subscription. The subscribers tend to be highly educated consumers. I thought these reports should not only be free but also that there needed to be aggressive outreach to senior citizens and the uninsured who were less sophisticated but desperately needed the information.

I rejected the Consumers Union proposal and urged them to develop a new plan. Within weeks, they returned with a strategy and budget for the free distribution of "Best Buy Drug" reports and an outreach program. The proposed budget was over $3 million for the first three years. The Engelberg Foundation agreed to fund the entire amount. To maintain the Consumers Union's credibility as an independent and unbiased source of consumer information, I agreed that I would have no input on which drugs would be studied or the substance of any reports. That didn't stop some PhRMA cronies from suggesting the project was biased because I was funding it.

Consumer Reports Best Buy Drugs was launched in December 2004. Sen. Hillary Clinton (D-NY) enthusiastically endorsed the program and gave the keynote speech at the launch event in Washington. The first three reports covered statins to reduce high cholesterol, drugs to treat acid reflux, and non-steroidal anti-inflammatory drugs for treating arthritis. Eventually, Best Buy Drugs reports were published for twenty-five of the most frequently prescribed classes of drugs. Best Buys were chosen based on a drug's effectiveness and safety, the side effects it might cause, how convenient it is to use, its track record in studies and use over time, and how much it costs relative to the other drugs. There was no set formula for choosing Best Buys. Best Buys were selected because they were as effective as all the other drugs in the category, or more so, had the same or fewer side effects and cost less. Despite being more expensive, several Best Buys were chosen for their superior effectiveness or safety profile.

In addition to publishing reports on its website, Consumers Union distributed two-page print versions in English and Spanish with the help of pharmacists, senior organizations, doctors, and libraries. Initially, outreach efforts were launched in five states. Groups that partnered with Best Buy Drugs to expand outreach efforts included the American Public Health Association, the Alliance for Retired Americans, the National Committee to Preserve Social Security and Medicare, the Association of American Medical Colleges, AARP, the National Urban League, the National Association of Area Agencies on Aging, National Center on Black Aged, and MGH Institute of Health Professions. During the ten-plus years that Best Buy Drugs operated, it received millions of dollars in additional funding from the National Library of Medicine, the National Institutes of Health, and the State Attorney General Consumer and Prescriber Education Grant Program.

Millions of patients used Best Buy Drug reports to select their medications, saving billions in medication costs. The program lasted for more than a decade before it ended. By then, all the me-too drugs used to treat chronic conditions were available as low-cost generics, and there was no longer a need to identify the "best buy." Millions of patients saved billions of dollars on their prescription drug costs because of Best Buy Drugs. I had made my fortune from generic drugs. I couldn't think of a better way to express gratitude than educating citizens to save money on the medicines they needed.

Ironically, the success of Best Buy Drugs deprived me of the opportunity to play a larger role in helping patients choose more affordable medicines. PhRMA used its influence to blackball me from being the founding chair of the Patient-Centered Outcomes Research Institute (PCORI).

PCORI was conceived to be an independent government entity conducting comparative clinical effectiveness research, which would be funded with close to $4 billion between 2010 and 2019 from a trust fund created by a small tax on private insurance and self-insured health plans and by transfers from Medicare and Medicaid. The authorization to create PCORI was buried in over two thousand pages of legislation that became the Affordable Care Act of 2010. PCORI would have an independent Board of Directors consisting of the Director of the Agency for Healthcare Research and Quality and the Director of the National Institutes of Health, or their designees, and nineteen members with diverse expertise in healthcare appointed for six-year terms by the Comptroller General.

Before it was formally born, what PCORI would do and how it would do it was controversial. Many legislators, egged on by PhRMA, opposed doing studies to compare two or more drugs or procedures. They feared it would eventually lead to denying insurance coverage for more expensive but less effective treatments. Others believed that an independent agency like PCORI was essential to eliminating wasteful spending. Similar institutions abroad were effective in doing so. The National Institute for Comparative Effectiveness (NICE) in the United Kingdom often recommended that the UK's National Health Service not cover drugs that were not cost-effective and was often successful in forcing drug companies to lower their prices based on comparative data.

I asked Senator Ron Wyden (D-OR) and Henry Waxman to urge Comptroller General Gene Dodaro to appoint me to the board of PCORI. They were both very enthusiastic about my willingness to serve. Dr. Kavita Patel, a Senior Fellow at Brookings and a former White House staffer who had worked on writing the enabling legislation for PCORI, was also instrumental in getting me considered. Within a couple of weeks, I had a telephone interview with a senior member of the Comptroller General's staff. She asked whether I would be willing to serve as PCORI's founding chairman. "Why me?" I asked. The answer was that most of the board members were likely to be medical professionals with no managerial or entrepreneurial skills. My background as a lawyer, entrepreneur, and philanthropist who had created initiatives such as the Engelberg Center on Health Care Reform at Brookings and Consumer Reports Best Buy Drugs made me a logical choice. I was flattered and expressed my willingness to serve. I knew it would be a full-time job to organize the board, hire key personnel, find office space, and get PCORI up and running. But it was a singular opportunity to define the culture of an organization that could save billions of dollars on drug costs by providing independent evaluations of new medicines.

By mid-August 2010, I had been advised that the Comptroller General would formally announce my appointment in late September. I was given two weeks to submit mountains of financial data to ensure no conflicts of interest existed. On Labor Day weekend, a Waxman staffer called to tell me I had been blackballed from the PCORI board. I was shocked and baffled. I naively thought the concept of "blackball" was limited to fraternity or social club membership. The staffer explained that the Comptroller General was a Congressional appointee and was accountable to Congress. It was standard practice to secretly share the names of potential appointees with the leadership of the relevant Senate committees before they were formally announced. My impending appointment as chair of PCORI was disclosed to the Senate Finance and Health Committees and leaked to PhRMA. Given my success in negotiating Hatch-Waxman and creating Consumer Reports Best Buy Drugs, it was no surprise that PhRMA would not want me to play any role in PCORI. They used their lobbying muscle to convince a Senator to use his power over the Comptroller General to "blackball" me. Although I could never confirm it, discussions with several senior congressional staffers led me to believe that my good friend Orrin Hatch was the blackballer. I didn't take it personally. It's just how politics works in Washington, even among friends. It's a favor a powerful Senator can deliver to his supporters without fear of adverse consequences.

Dr. Eugene Washington, then the dean of UCLA Medical School and now the CEO of the Duke University Health System, was appointed chair of PCORI on September 23, 2010. In November 2012, while still serving in that capacity, Washington joined the board of Johnson & Johnson. It was a serious conflict of interest. Yet he remained the chair of PCORI until the end of 2013. In 2016, the Center for American Progress reviewed PCORI's effectiveness in conducting and disseminating comparative effectiveness research. It found that only 4.4 percent ($60 million) of the $1.4 billion in research grants made by PCORI had gone to studies comparing two or more drugs.

The issue today is not simply whether one drug is better than another but whether medicines that are now routinely priced at $100,000 per patient or more produce a benefit for patients that is worth their price. Agencies like NICE in the UK or the Institute for Clinical and Economic Review in the United States are doing important evaluations of the true value of a new drug that can be useful in negotiating a fairer price. PCORI should be at the forefront of this work. It isn't. But it would have been had I been the founding chair.

Unfortunately, the PCORI incident is not an isolated example of how PhRMA money has undermined my efforts to make healthcare more affordable and accessible. The Brookings Institution has long been among the world's most prestigious think tanks and policy influencers. I first met Brookings CEO Strobe Talbott in 2004. In 2007, after extensive discussions with Strobe and the leading healthcare economists at Brookings, I agreed to fund the creation of the Engelberg Center on Health Care Reform at Brookings with a grant of $10 million. My goal was to stimulate a national dialogue on reducing healthcare costs by developing new methods of payment that emphasized primary care and paying for episodes of care rather than paying a fee for each service. Although I am a lifelong Democrat, I urged Strobe to hire Mark McClellan as the Engelberg Center's director even though he was serving in the administration of George W. Bush. I didn't know him personally, but I was familiar with his advocacy for payment reform and his reputation as a leader in healthcare policy.

From my first meeting with Mark, it was clear that he was a thoroughly political animal. He was a Texas Republican, but his primary interest seemed to be how to position himself to become the next Secretary of Health regardless of whether a Democrat or a Republican was elected president. He was careful in expressing his policy beliefs so they would be palatable to both ends of the political spectrum. Mark wanted to simultaneously serve as a fellow at the American Enterprise Institute, a conservative think tank, while leading the Engelberg Center at Brookings. I had reservations about Mark's personality and collegiality from our initial meeting, but I still felt he was the best person for the job.

Hiring Mark was a mistake that became obvious early in his tenure. He ran the Engelberg Center like a political operation rather than a collegial think tank. The fellows were not free to pursue any ideas of their own, participate in forums, publish papers, or even talk to the media without preclearance from Mark. He did not participate in the usual intellectual exchanges with other Brookings scholars in economic studies, some of whom were also engaged in work related to healthcare financing. Mark was invisible. He ran the Engelberg Center through a chief of staff, Larry Kocot, who guarded his calendar and door and enforced his edicts. Mark was difficult to reach and was often away giving speeches for money or consulting. No other scholar or senior official at Brookings operated in such a high-handed fashion, and it caused an endless stream of management issues and turnover.

Despite these problems, McClellan was instrumental in making the Engelberg Center a key player in the healthcare reform discussions leading to the enactment of Obamacare and its implementation. His series of papers and forums on "Bending the Curve" on healthcare costs became a significant part of the national discussion on controlling costs. He was also a leader in new payment models and championed creating Accountable Care Organizations (ACOs). ACOs were an effort to duplicate the success of integrated closed network providers like Kaiser, where all the doctors and specialists are on salary and work together to coordinate a patient's care.

McClellan's work vaulted Brookings to the top rankings nationally as a healthcare think tank. That was all that mattered to Strobe Talbott, and it was enough to prevent him from doing anything about McClellan's poor management of the Engelberg Center. The bottom line seemed to be that Brookings needed Mark more than Mark needed Brookings. That became painfully apparent when McClellan announced in 2013 that he had joined the board of directors of Johnson & Johnson. Brookings allows its scholars to supplement their incomes by working 20 percent of their time on outside activities like teaching, consulting, or giving paid speeches, provided those activities are precleared by Brookings management and don't conflict with Brookings' reputation as an independent policy-making organization. McClellan had failed to seek preclearance for joining Johnson & Johnson despite the obvious conflict of interest between his new fiduciary obligation to a major drug company and the independence required to lead a Brookings health policy program. Yet Strobe and the Brookings management team did not require McClellan to choose between his board seat or his employment at Brookings. I was livid! Given my roots in the generic drug industry, it was a slap in the face and a personal embarrassment for me.

To add insult to injury, not long afterward, in October 2014, McClellan scheduled a public program at Brookings to discuss high drug prices and how to pay for them. It was just after the introduction of the hepatitis C drug, Sovaldi, at $89,000 per patient. The program was led by Dana Goldman of the Schaeffer Center at USC and Tomas Philipson, a conservative economist from the University of Chicago who later became Trump's chief economic advisor. I was a panelist on the program and a solitary voice for the assertion that drugs were overpriced. During the program, Philipson suggested that the high cost of Sovaldi was merely a credit issue that could easily be resolved if patients took out a second mortgage on their homes so they could pay for the drug over time. It was absurd! Neither Goldman nor Philipson disclosed that, in addition to their academic appointments, they were partners in Precision Health Economics, a highly profitable consulting firm for large pharmaceutical companies. They were being paid to do studies favorable to the pharmaceutical industry's interests and published under their academic credentials to create the false appearance that the studies were unbiased. I was aware of their conflict and expressed disappointment that Brookings would provide its prestigious platform for presenting views sponsored by pharmaceutical companies without full disclosure.

When Strobe Talbott informed me that he was in discussions to create a joint venture between the USC Schaeffer Center and the Engelberg Center to raise additional funding, it was the last straw for me. I resigned from the Brookings board and removed my name from the Engelberg Center in 2015. Two years later, *ProPublica* exposed that PhRMA companies were paying Precision Health Economics to have Goldman, Philipson, and others publish academic articles favorable to their drugs without disclosing that they were paid to write them.

It was a bitter disappointment to realize that it's always about money in Washington, whether you are a legislator or a think tank. Think tanks claim to be independent, but operating in expensive quarters with well-paid scholars requires tens of millions of dollars annually. You can't raise that much money from people who disagree with your ideas. But you can get big gifts from those who want to misuse the prestige of your think tank to promote their own interests.

I am optimistic about the future of another major philanthropic effort that is a direct outgrowth of my experience negotiating the Hatch-Waxman Act. One of the earliest grants made by the Engelberg Foundation was motivated by what I saw as the shortcomings in the process that led to the enactment of Hatch-Waxman. It didn't seem right that important legislation should result from a negotiation between the commercially interested parties with no real input from independent experts representing the public interest. John Sexton, the charismatic dean of NYU School of Law in the early '90s, convinced me to get involved with my alma mater and solicited me for a major gift. We spent many hours discussing my career and my role in Hatch-Waxman. One outcome of those discussions was the recognition that the leading law schools had overlooked the importance of intellectual property law as a field of scholarly inquiry despite the importance of innovation to the economy. Many elite law schools didn't even offer a course in patent law. Yet every major law school had many scholars in constitutional, administrative, criminal, and other fields of law.

The Engelberg Center on Innovation Law & Policy at NYU Law School was born from those discussions. We agreed that NYU should lead by creating a center where faculty, scholars, students, and invited participants could conduct research, author papers, host seminars, provide expert testimony to Congress, and stimulate scholarship and discussion of emerging innovation law and policy issues. In its early years, I urged the Center to avoid getting involved in matters related to implementing Hatch-Waxman or pharmaceutical patent monopolies. I feared the Center would fail to develop a reputation as a credible venue for independent scholarship if people thought I had created it as a platform to advocate my personal views.

The Center is now well-established as a national leader in intellectual property law. It has a prestigious board of advisors consisting of judges, scholars, corporate intellectual property law department leaders, and law firm partners engaged in intellectual property law practices who help set its agenda and participate in its programs.

Chapter Eleven

SOUNDING THE ALARM ON POLICIES RESPONSIBLE FOR THE HIGH COST OF PRESCRIPTION DRUGS

HATCH-WAXMAN AND THE BPCIA HAVE failed to stimulate greater private investment in research to discover new medicines, but they have succeeded in making new drugs far more expensive and drug monopolies far longer. I have published many articles on this important subject, several of which (including "How Government Policy Promotes High Drug Prices," *Health Affairs Forefront*, October 29, 2015; "Memo to the President: The Pharmaceutical Monopoly Adjustment Act Of 2017," *Health Affairs Forefront*, September 13, 2016; "A Shortfall in Innovation is the Cause of High Drug Prices," *Health Affairs Forefront*, February 28, 2019; "Unaffordable Prescription Drugs: The Real Legacy of the Hatch-Waxman Act," *STAT*, December 16, 2020; and "Clearing the Patent Thicket: A Pathway to Faster Generic Drug Approvals," *STAT*, March 10, 2023) explain why the laws making generic drugs more available have failed to lower overall drug spending.

A generation of rapid revenue growth for branded pharmaceuticals began to subside around 2009 because the patent monopolies on many blockbuster drugs were expiring. Between 2009 and 2017, patent expirations resulted in a loss of $185 billion in brand-name drug sales. Pharmaceutical manufacturers did not introduce enough new drugs to replace that lost revenue. Most of the new drugs being launched were specialty drugs taken by relatively small patient populations compared to the millions of patients who took a blockbuster drug to treat high cholesterol, hypertension, reflux, and depression. Even though these specialty drugs were launched at much higher prices than the blockbuster drugs, they produced less revenue. The increased use of generic drugs due to patent expirations should have significantly reduced overall spending on prescription drugs. It did not. According to the IQVIA annual reports on pharmaceutical sales, revenue grew by $140 billion even though the number of prescriptions filled with a brand-name drug dropped by more than 50 percent from 910 million to 425 million prescriptions annually.

The IQVIA data establishes that price increases on existing brand-name drugs account for all of the growth in revenue for brand-name drug manufacturers. Total price increases for the period amounted to $187 billion, offsetting the revenue losses from patent expirations. Brand-name drug manufacturers routinely imposed annual price increases on existing drugs by 10 percent or more.

As a result of high launch prices and aggressive price increases, spending on the twenty bestselling branded drugs in 2018 was greater than the total sales of all generic drugs: $109 billion versus $103 billion. Five of the twelve bestselling branded drugs had already enjoyed at least twenty years of monopoly protection, and three others fifteen years or more. Between 2012 and 2017, four best-selling drugs had cumulative price increases of more than 100 percent: Lyrica, 166 percent; Enbrel, 155 percent; Humira, 144 percent; and Lantus, 114 percent.

The bottom line is that Hatch-Waxman succeeded beyond all expectations in making low-cost generic drugs widely available. Ninety percent of prescriptions in the United States, over five billion per year, are filled with a generic drug. Yet the 10 percent market share of patented medicines accounts for 82.5 percent of prescription drug spending. The savings that should have resulted from the dramatic increase in generic drug prescriptions have gone into the pockets of brand-name drug manufacturers due to higher prices for patented drugs. In 2016, Len Schleifer, the CEO of Regeneron Pharmaceuticals, aptly stated: "We as an industry have used price increases to cover up the gaps in innovation." That is an understatement. Hatch-Waxman and the BPCIA covering biologic medicines were supposed to produce more innovation while lowering prescription drug costs. Instead, they resulted in less innovation and higher prices. Congress failed to recognize that while generic competition is essential to assuring reasonable drug prices after monopolies expire, total spending on medicines is determined by how long the monopolies last and the prices charged while those monopolies exist.

Before Hatch-Waxman, brand-name drug manufacturers argued that the remaining patent life when a new drug was approved was too short, about eight years. That argument was based on the false assertion that monopoly protection for a new drug ended when the patent claiming the new drug molecule expired. In truth, a broken patent system coupled with a loophole created by Hatch-Waxman allows brand-name drug manufacturers to not only acquire patents claiming trivial changes made to a drug after it is approved, but also assert those patents to wrongfully delay legitimate generic competition for many years after the patent claiming the new drug molecule has expired.

The patent certification provisions of Hatch-Waxman prohibit the FDA from approving a competing generic drug for thirty months whenever a patent infringement claim is asserted. The delay is worth billions in extra monopoly profits. It incentivizes piling up meritless secondary patents. Yet, as my experience in challenging patents proves, most trivial patents do not survive patent challenges. Over ten thousand Hatch-Waxman patent challenges have been filed since the law was enacted, and several hundred new challenges are filed annually. A Hatch-Waxman ANDA Litigation Forum on LinkedIn has over fourteen thousand members, and drug patent challenges are now a major legal subspecialty.

Brand-name manufacturers have learned that acquiring bad patents is good business because the existence of a bad patent delays competition and keeps drug prices and profits high. Generic manufacturers have learned that a successful patent challenge produces far greater profits than selling a low-margin generic drug in a highly competitive market. The bottom line is that the patent certification system created by Hatch-Waxman provides an incentive to game the patent system, which is highly profitable for both brand and generic manufacturers. It is bad for the public, which pays higher prices for longer periods because of unwarranted monopolies.

The Hatch-Waxman Act did not require patent certifications for secondary patents. Under the specific language of Hatch-Waxman, only the patent "...which claims the drug for which the applicant submitted the application..." or the use for which approval is sought was eligible for the thirty-month injunction. Only the basic patents eligible for a patent term extension under Hatch-Waxman were eligible for listing in the FDA Orange Book as patents for which certification was required. Unfortunately, in promulgating regulations to implement Hatch-Waxman, the FDA disregarded the specific language of the law and required all patents that claim "...the drug that is the subject of the NDA or amendment or supplement to it..." to be listed in the FDA Orange Book. That opened the door to listing patents covering changes made to the drug after the NDA was submitted or approved and incentivized the creation of patent thickets. A study by Bhaven Sampat and his colleagues shows that the average number of patents per drug went from 1.9 for drugs approved between 1985 and 1987 to 6.1 for drugs approved between 2012 and 2014, an increase of 321 percent.

Under FDA law, changes to a new drug made after it is approved may not change the safety or efficacy of a drug. A generic applicant should be free to copy the originally approved drug without incorporating the immaterial changes a belated patent covers. The belated patent is irrelevant. As a matter of patent law, a belated patent cannot be infringed by copying the originally approved drug on which patent protection has expired. You can't patent the same thing twice. Therefore, there is no reasonable basis for requiring certification for a belated patent.

Unfortunately, the FDA has no expertise in patent law, as it has repeatedly admitted. Congress should never have delegated authority to the FDA to enact and enforce regulations interpreting the patent provisions of the Hatch-Waxman Act. Its failure to follow the letter of the law has allowed thousands of ineligible patents to be wrongfully listed in the FDA Orange Book to delay legitimate generic competition. It has dramatically inflated the cost of medicines.

Unlike the situation with Hatch-Waxman, Congress deliberately created much longer and stronger monopoly protections for biologic drugs covered by the BPCIA and encouraged patent thickets. It gave new biologic drugs twelve years of guaranteed exclusivity even without patents. After that, the owner of an approved biologic can assert any patent it owns to delay competition from a generic version. It doesn't matter if the patent was granted after the brand-name drug was approved or whether it covers any aspect of the approved drug. Protracted litigation over a patent thicket consisting of dozens (sometimes hundreds) of manufacturing patents granted after the new biologic was approved makes it possible for monopolies on commercially important biologic drugs to easily last more than twenty years.

Worse yet, there is currently no true generic market for biologics. Most generic biologics are approved as "biosimilar." That means they are not automatically interchangeable with the original product and cannot be automatically substituted on prescriptions written for the branded drug under state substitution laws. Many doctors are reluctant to switch patients to a different drug if their current medication works. That means biosimilars do not quickly displace demand for the original biologic and therefore must be marketed to physicians like me-too drugs. Biosimilars are also relatively expensive. Small molecule generics typically sell at a 90 percent discount from the brand-name price; biosimilars typically sell at less than a 50 percent discount.

The bottom line is that a drug price crisis exists because the government permits the owners of FDA-approved drugs to enjoy longer monopolies and does little or nothing to rein in prices and price increases while those monopolies exist. As a result, patented drug prices are three to four times higher in the United States than in Europe, and per capita spending on drugs is twice the average cost in Europe, even though generic drug use is much higher here.

Another major issue that I have written about is the government's failure to achieve more reasonable prices for the growing number of drugs discovered as a result of federally funded research grants. In "Commentary: Taxpayers are entitled to reasonable prices on federally funded drug discoveries," *Modern Healthcare*, July 18, 2018, "Do large pharma companies provide drug development innovation? Our analysis says no," Emily H. Jung, Alfred Engelberg, and Aaron S. Kesselheim, *STAT*, December 10, 2019, and "A New Way to Contain Unaffordable Medication Costs—Exercising the Government's Existing

Rights," Alfred B. Engelberg, JD, Jerry Avorn, MD, and Aaron S. Kesselheim, MD, JD, MPH, *New England Journal of Medicine*, February 9, 2022, I called attention to government studies showing that pharmaceutical companies no longer do basic research. Instead, they rely on the government's $50 billion annual investment in basic biomedical research, which the National Institute of Health distributes to the nation's academic medical centers and universities. The large pharmaceutical companies have become investment banks and earn the lion's share of their revenue from selling drugs acquired from third parties.

In the private sector, the patents and trade secrets flowing from research investments are owned by the party that pays for the research. However, under the Bayh-Dole Act of 1980, the patent rights flowing from federally funded research are given to the universities and their inventors without significant restrictions on how they may exploit these rights. They can sell the rights to pharmaceutical companies or start their own companies. Either way, neither the government nor taxpayers get any discount on the price of a drug because of their financial contribution to its discovery. The government does receive a paid-up royalty-free license to use the patented invention for government purposes. It has never used that license to produce a low-cost generic drug for government health insurance programs, even though the Government Accountability Office has stated it is free to do so.

Xtandi, a drug for treating advanced prostate cancer, is a recent example of a federally funded drug discovery that has been turned into an overpriced drug. It was discovered at UCLA, and the patent rights were transferred to Medivation, a start-up created by the inventors. Medivation formed a joint venture with Astellas, a Japanese pharmaceutical company, and the drug was sold for $125,000 per patient annually. Subsequently, Pfizer acquired ownership of Xtandi for $14 billion and raised the price to $189,000, about $90/pill. Xtandi costs Medicare about $2 billion a year. Biolyse Pharma has offered to sell the government a generic version of Xtandi for $3/pill. Yet NIH, without explanation, refuses to exercise the government's royalty-free license to manufacture a generic version of Xtandi. No law allows NIH to revoke the government's license or prevent its use. Even without the license, the government is immune from patent infringement claims. The license simply shields the government from any claim for additional compensation.

Taxpayers are paying twice. First, to fund the cost and risk involved in the discovery of new drugs, and second, when they are compelled to pay an exorbitant price for the drug to provide companies like Pfizer with windfall profits. This is not free market capitalism. The government has socialized the cost and risk of drug discovery and privatized the profits. A new paradigm is needed that provides reasonable economic incentives for private investment in the commercial development of federally funded discoveries while recognizing the taxpayers' right to fair pricing in return for the investment that led to the discovery of the drug.

The failure of the free market has also unfairly driven up the cost of generic drugs while simultaneously forcing many generic drug manufacturers out of business. The result has been critical shortages of many older drugs and massive price spikes for others. I began calling attention to these issues many years ago in "Addressing Generic Drug Unaffordability and Shortages by Globalizing the Market For Old Drugs," *Health Affairs Forefront*, February 23, 2016; "The VA Pharmacy Benefit Manager Should Take Over the Operation of Medicare Part D," *Health Affairs*, April 20, 2018; and "Outdated rule increases Medicare's costs for generic drugs by $26 billion a year", *STAT*, September 10, 2021.

Examples of this include the 5,000 percent increase in Daraprim from thirteen dollars to $750 orchestrated by Turing Pharmaceuticals and Martin Shkreli and the 500 percent price increase imposed by Mylan for a generic EpiPen, both of which received sensational media coverage. Yet many other price spike cases received no publicity. In every case, the cause was the same. The generic manufacturer had no competition and raised the price to whatever level the market would bear, the same pricing strategy that brand-name manufacturers routinely use in pricing patented medicines. Yet public outrage seems to be much higher when price gouging results from a price increase on an old drug rather than a high price for a new drug. Consumers assume that free market capitalism always produces optimum competition to keep prices reasonable. It turns out to not be that simple in a regulated industry where the ability of manufacturers to enter a market rapidly does not exist because FDA approval takes a long time.

Antitrust regulators stood idly by while AmerisourceBergen, McKesson, and Cardinal Health gained control of over 90 percent of the wholesale distribution of drugs, seven companies operating pharmacies—CVS Health, Walgreens Boots Alliance, Cigna, UnitedHealth Group, Walmart, Kroger, and Rite Aid—gained control of 70 percent of the prescription drug dispensing market, and hospitals formed large buying groups. Eventually, the number of generic manufacturers greatly exceeded the number of buyers, which drove down prices and profit margins for generic drugs. Many generic manufacturers merged, were driven out of business, or discontinued unprofitable product lines.

When only a few sellers remain, the situation reverses. A supply chain disruption, quality control problem, FDA compliance issue, or a combination of these factors can create a drug shortage or a monopoly. The active ingredient of most generic drugs comes from abroad, often from China or India. Supply disruptions have become more common, especially during the COVID-19 pandemic. Many manufacturers have closed their doors due to failed FDA inspections and a lack of capital to upgrade facilities. Sometimes, the FDA exacerbates the problem by demanding upgrades to manufacturing facilities to incorporate the latest technologies to ensure product purity and quality. The bottom line is that hundreds of small-volume generic drugs, particularly injectable drugs, manufactured in complex sterile manufacturing facilities have had enormous price increases due to monopolies. In other cases, a drug is not available at any price.

Group buyers now realize they made a mistake in driving generic drug prices down to the point where too many manufacturers were forced out of business. Shortages and price increases have wiped out any savings and endangered lives. Some healthcare systems and philanthropies have recently banded together to create Civica Rx, a not-for-profit entity that manufactures generic drugs in chronic short supply. It's a good idea, but it takes time and capital investment. The hundreds of drug shortages that now exist are not going to be resolved by a single entity. Many drugs in short supply in the US are available in other countries. The FDA must make it easier for US purchasers to access these sources by expediting the generic drug approval process. Buyers need to assure foreign suppliers of long-term access to the market at reasonable prices, given the past practice of buying groups to slash prices to unprofitable levels for manufacturers.

Generic drug prices have also been inflated by pharmacy benefit managers (PBMs). PBMs served a useful purpose in reducing drug costs during the era when several drugs were available to treat the same condition, and some were expensive branded products while others were available as low-cost generics. They helped insurance companies to keep drug spending down just as Consumer Reports Best Buy Drugs did for senior citizens. But, in recent years, they have misused their position as middlemen in the drug selection process and the lack of transparency about the enormous price differential between brand and generic drugs to produce more profit for themselves rather than savings for those who use their services.

In 2022, Mark Cuban made headlines when he launched the Mark Cuban Cost Plus Drug Company, which fills prescriptions at a small mark-up from the drug's acquisition cost plus a dispensing fee instead of the much higher markups charged by PBMs. There is nothing new about that approach. I had addressed it years earlier in some of my cited articles. Those articles provided comparative data showing that the prices paid for generic drugs by Medicare are far higher than the Veterans Administration's costs for the same drugs because the VA operates its own PBM. The data also showed that Costco, Amazon, and other low-cost sellers have profitably offered patients hundreds of generic prescriptions for four dollars or less. They make a reasonable profit despite the low selling price because the acquisition cost of the pills in a thirty-day prescription is only fifty or sixty cents, and the dispensing cost is less than three dollars.

Medicare doesn't need a complex insurance system run by PBMs to pay for the generic drugs used to fill 90 percent of all Medicare prescriptions. Indeed, it is now often cheaper for patients to pay for a drug without using their Medicare Part D insurance because the co-payment is higher than the cash price for the same prescription without insurance. I estimated that Medicare could save $18 billion annually if it redesigned the Part D benefit and paid pharmacists directly. Patients would save an additional $8 billion they are now shelling out in out-of-pocket co-payments for generic drugs. That doesn't make any sense. Fortunately, Congress is now belatedly waking up to the extra cost burden being needlessly imposed by the unfair business practices of PBMs and is considering legislation to address the problem.

Chapter Twelve

MY PRESCRIPTION FOR THE FUTURE

We are at the beginning of another golden age for pharmaceuticals. Genomic science, the ability to edit genes, and the use of artificial intelligence tools to accelerate drug discovery hold the promise of finding more effective treatments and cures for many conditions. But these drugs must be affordable. Unaffordable drugs may be worse for society than not discovering them at all. Policymakers claimed that Hatch-Waxman and the BPCIA would balance affordability and the incentive to invest in discovering new drugs by creating pathways for robust generic competition. Experience proves that generic competition is insufficient to rein in the cost of medicines. Drug spending is a function of how long the monopoly on a new drug lasts and the prices charged while the monopoly exists. To reduce drug spending to affordable levels, we need new laws that:

1. Limit the length of a monopoly on a new drug to the life of the basic patent claiming the drug or its approved use.
2. Rein in drug prices while a new drug enjoys monopoly protection.
3. Assure taxpayers pay reasonable prices for drugs discovered with government funding.
4. Assure that generic drugs are available to patients at a fair price.

1. LIMITING MONOPOLIES

To anyone other than a patent attorney, the notion that you cannot copy a drug after the patent claiming the drug expires defies common sense. So does the idea that an immaterial change to an approved new drug can delay legitimate competition after the basic patent claiming the active ingredient of the new drug has expired. Yet Hatch-Waxman and the BPCIA routinely delay generic and biosimilar competition for many years after the basic patent claiming a drug expires. The public interest requires strict enforcement of a "one and done" policy, which ensures that a new drug gets one monopoly, and competition begins on the day that monopoly ends.

There are several ways to achieve that goal without major changes to existing law. Yet experience shows that unless laws are written with absolute clarity, self-interested parties will find loopholes to make monopolies last longer. Therefore, the simplest solution might be to repeal all existing laws governing pharmaceutical monopolies and write a new one that gives a new drug a fixed number of years of monopoly with no exceptions. A definitive new law would eliminate the time, energy, and money now wasted on efforts by pharmaceutical companies to extend and by generic manufacturers to shorten the life of drug monopolies. There is no greater incentive to discover a new drug than the looming expiration of a monopoly on a profitable existing drug. A fixed and immovable date for that monopoly's expiration would encourage the development of new drugs to replace the revenues lost to generic competition when the monopoly on the old drug expires.

There are two problems with this approach. First, the Constitution guarantees the right to a patent. All patent rights would have to be waived in exchange for the guaranteed monopoly. Second, pharmaceutical manufacturers are unlikely to voluntarily waive their patent rights unless the guaranteed monopoly bears a reasonable relationship to the potential length of a patent monopoly. All new biologic drugs now receive a guaranteed monopoly of twelve years. As a practical political matter, that would have to be the minimum length of a guaranteed monopoly. Should it be longer for a breakthrough drug than a me-too drug with little or no advantage over an existing treatment? Should it be shorter if the drug was discovered under a federal research grant? In all likelihood, the guaranteed monopoly would have to range from twelve to fifteen years.

A less drastic way to limit monopolies is to repeal the FDA regulations implementing Hatch-Waxman that permit belated secondary patents to block FDA approval of generic drugs. No patent claiming changes made to a new drug after it has been approved should be eligible for the patent certification process of Hatch-Waxman. That was the original intent of the law. The current FDA regulation that compels the identification of secondary patents related to changes made to an approved drug violates both the language and intent of Hatch-Waxman, and it exceeds the FDA's authority to promulgate regulations implementing the law.

Limiting the availability of patent certification to the basic patents would eliminate the ability of secondary patents to trigger the automatic thirty-month delay in the FDA's approval of a generic drug. That would drastically reduce the number of patent challenges and agreements between brand-name and generic manufacturers to settle those challenges by delaying generic competition.

There is a potential downside to eliminating patent challenges to secondary patents. Generic manufacturers might become vulnerable to patent infringement claims and damages for infringing trivial secondary patents after they commercially launch a competing generic drug. Two changes to current law would significantly reduce that possibility and ensure that generic applicants have a pathway for avoiding infringement.

First, the owner of an approved new drug or new biologic application should continue to be required to identify all patents claiming changes to the drug or biologic that might be infringed if the approved drug is copied. Those patents should still be listed in the FDA Orange Book or the Purple Book for approved biologics even though no certification is required.

Second, applicants filing supplements to make changes to a new drug or biologic should be required to certify that the change does not alter the approved drug's safety, efficacy, or bioequivalence and need not be copied to produce a bioequivalent generic copy. Such a certification is consistent with current FDA regulations that bar material changes to an approved drug. If a change is material, it should not be permitted. If it is not material, it should not be necessary for a generic applicant to copy the change to gain approval. If the FDA consistently applied these rules, trivial secondary patents would never be infringed, and patent thickets could never delay legitimate competition or create potential infringement liability.

Amendments to Hatch-Waxman will not reduce the use of trivial secondary patents to prolong monopolies over biologic drugs. The BPCIA should be amended to mirror Hatch-Waxman's patent disclosure and certification requirements. The BPCIA, as originally enacted, has no patent certification procedure or limits on what patents may be asserted. Instead, Congress created a "gotcha" game where a generic (biosimilar) applicant can be sued for infringing patents that did not exist when a new biologic drug was approved. Those patents don't have to be identified until an application for biosimilar approval is filed, often many years after the new biologic drug has been approved. These overly generous provisions of the BPCIA were based on the false premise that biotech start-ups needed extra incentives to attract capital. Most of these start-ups are based on patents developed with federal funding. Yet monopolies for federally funded biologic inventions now routinely last twenty years or more and typically cost tens of thousands annually per patient.

Congress should also amend the BPCIA to require brand-name drug manufacturers to fully disclose the content of their application for the approved biologic in exchange for the twelve-year monopoly they now automatically receive for every new biologic drug. The branded biologic drug continues to enjoy the lion's share of the market after all its monopolies end because the approved generic product is biosimilar rather than interchangeable with the branded product. It is not automatically substitutable under state generic substitution laws. Patent thickets would be useless, and the public would benefit from robust generic competition between equivalent products if the law allowed generic competitors to exactly copy the approved biologic. The twelve-year exclusivity for new biologics was based on the theory that the manufacturers of new biologics were entitled to a property right in the data and information submitted for approval of their new drug. The logical quid pro quo for that exclusivity is full disclosure of that information so the public receives a benefit in exchange for the monopoly.

In an ideal world, the Patent Office would not grant so many worthless patents, and creating patent thickets to prolong monopolies would not be possible. Yet the problem defies all efforts to fix it. It is time to accept that a patent system that depends on highly subjective decisions by examiners with little or no real-world experience and insufficient time to spend on each patent application cannot turn out a high-quality product. While admirable, the efforts of I-Mak and other consumer groups to reform the patent examination system will not materially alter a system that has resisted all efforts to change it during the more than sixty years since I served as a patent examiner. We should stop pretending otherwise and modify our patent laws to reflect reality.

An arcane rule of patent law states that a patent is presumed valid, and a court cannot declare a patent invalid without clear and convincing evidence. The "clear and convincing" standard is akin to the "beyond a reasonable doubt" standard of proof that applies to criminal cases. It is so high that the same evidence that would have caused a patent examiner to deny the patent before it is granted is insufficient to invalidate it afterward. These rules defy common sense. A patent examiner spends an average of less than twenty hours, including searching for prior patents and publications, before granting a patent. Patent challengers hire scientific experts and spend hundreds of hours and large sums of money to find far more compelling evidence about what others knew when a patent was sought. Patent trials always involve a much more comprehensive body of evidence on what others already knew before, the differences between what was known and what is claimed in the patent, and the level of skill in the field of the invention. A preponderance of the evidence should similarly determine whether a patent is valid, which is the same standard used in other civil litigation.

Recently, the US Supreme Court overturned the decades-old Chevron deference that presumed the correctness of decisions made by federal agencies based on their expertise. A determination by the Patent Office that a patent is valid should not be entitled to any deference.

Without a presumption of validity, trivial patents claiming minor changes to a drug would rarely survive scrutiny. Changes made to a new drug after the FDA approves it are only permitted when the change is so minor that it has no material effect on the safety or efficacy of a drug. That should be sufficient to prove that the change is not worthy of patent protection. But, under current law, if the applicant tells the patent examiner that the change produces a new or unexpected result, the examiner routinely grants the patent. Courts routinely strike down patents when the patent applicant tells the FDA that a change is trivial so that the FDA permits it but simultaneously tells a patent examiner that the change produces an unexpected result of sufficient magnitude to be unobvious and merit patent protection. But in the bizarre world of patent law, the presumption of validity puts the burden on the patent challenger to present clear and convincing evidence to overcome the presumption of validity even in situations where the applicant made misrepresentations to the Patent Office.

Patent thickets would also wither if the remedy for infringing a secondary drug patent was limited to monetary damages and courts were prohibited from granting injunctions against future infringement. In *eBay Inc. v. MercExchange, L.L.C.* (547 US 388 (2006)), the Supreme Court held that an injunction for patent infringement is discretionary and should not be granted when it would do a disservice to the public interest. In enacting Hatch-Waxman, Congress declared a vital public interest in assuring that generic competition would begin when the basic patents claiming an FDA-approved drug expired. Delaying generic competition after that because of a secondary patent claiming a minor change is a clear disservice to the public interest. Congress could modify the statutory remedies available for patent infringement and eliminate the possibility of injunctive relief for trivial secondary patents instead of leaving judges free to make that determination case-by-case.

Patent law already provides that damages for infringement of a secondary patent claiming an alleged improvement must exclude the value of the unimproved product on which patent protection has expired. Trivial improvements should result in trivial damage awards. Without the threat of an injunction, damages for infringement of secondary patents would be less than the cost of litigation to enforce them.

The Hatch-Waxman Act was based on a lie that PhRMA sold to Congress. That lie was that the monopoly over a new drug ended when the basic patent claiming the active ingredient of the new drug or its medical use expired. I called out that lie, to no avail, in testimony before Congress in 1982 and in an article in *Health Affairs* that year. Forty years later, it has become clear that the length of a monopoly on a new drug is determined by "product life cycle management," PhRMA's euphemism for manipulating patents and the FDA by making trivial changes to a new drug after it is approved to prolong the monopoly. It's time to end product life cycle management and amend the laws to give PhRMA what it said it wanted—a monopoly of reasonable length on a new drug that ends when the basic patent claiming the new drug expires.

2. REINING IN PRICES

The Inflation Reduction Act of 2022 (IRA) is the first serious effort to lower the sky-high prices of patented drugs. It was prompted by the realization that existing law prohibiting the government from directly negotiating drug prices under Medicare Part D led to US prices that were three or four times higher than the price for the same drug in Europe. The IRA authorizes the government to negotiate lower prices for Medicare Part D drugs. The first ten drugs subject to negotiation have been selected, and the price reductions will take effect in 2026. Price reductions for additional drugs will be negotiated annually after that. Despite claims by the PhRMA lobby that the IRA will result in a devastating reduction in biomedical innovation, the Congressional Budget Office calculates that only thirteen fewer new drugs (1 percent) will reach the market between 2023 and 2032 and seven fewer in the following decade.

The Part D price negotiations are not likely to provide much relief from high drug prices and come too late. A 50 percent reduction in current Part D prices will not even bring Part D prices down to the net prices paid for the same drugs by Medicaid or the Veterans Administration. That is because drug price increases in those programs have long been capped at the rate of inflation, while drug prices in Medicare Part D have been rising rapidly because of aggressive annual price increases since the program began in 2006.

The price of the twenty-five most expensive drugs in Part D has tripled since they were introduced. If the inflation cap had been in place when Medicare Part D began in 2006, over $100 billion would already have been saved, and the net cost of those drugs would be the same as in Medicaid and other government programs. The Inflation Reduction Act also limits future price increases on Medicare Part D drugs to the rate of inflation. That provision may have the greatest long-term impact.

Contract clauses capping price increases by suppliers at the inflation rate are common in procurement contracts in both the public and private sectors. It is a mystery that they are not routinely required by insurance companies or large corporations that provide prescription drug coverage for tens of millions of employees. The likely answer is that the profitability of the PBMs that administer prescription drug benefits for most private sector health plans benefit from higher drug prices. Higher drug prices produce larger rebates and create the illusion that PBMs are holding down drug spending in the face of higher prices. But the rebates are meaningless if total net spending on drugs continues to rise, especially when the share of prescriptions filled with a low-cost generic drug is also rising.

Congress is unlikely to consider additional laws to reduce drug prices before the impact of the Part D negotiations is known in 2026. Depending on which way the political winds blow in the 2024 election cycle, it is more likely that we will see efforts to repeal Part D price negotiations. There is also a risk that pending legal challenges to the IRA by the pharmaceutical industry could succeed. But that risk seems small given the decisions rendered by the courts so far. Those decisions have emphasized that participation in the price negotiation process authorized by the IRA is voluntary. Pharmaceutical manufacturers can withdraw from the

Medicare program if they don't want to negotiate lower prices. Few, if any, are likely to do so, given the size of the Medicare program and the expectation that negotiated prices will still produce significant profits.

Any additional efforts to lower drug prices must come from the states or the private sector. Balanced budget laws make it increasingly difficult for states to cover the cost of high-priced drugs. The introduction of drugs like Sovaldi to treat hepatitis C forced rationing. The GLP-1 weight loss drugs are likely to create a similar crisis since there are tens of millions of obese patients with diabetes, heart disease, or some other condition that would benefit from these drugs. At $10,000 per patient annually, the cost of these drugs could be hundreds of billions annually, and many of the patients are in state Medicaid programs.

Prescription drug affordability boards have been created in several states as an avenue for capping drug prices. However, they face legal challenges from the pharmaceutical industry, and the outcome remains to be determined. States certainly have a role in protecting their citizens from price gouging. One solution is for states to define price gouging to include drug price increases that exceed the inflation rate and are not justified by cost. Some may argue that eliminating price increases on prescription drugs will result in higher launch prices. That is unlikely. Experience proves that the uptake of expensive new drugs is slow and is impacted by price. Historically, pharmaceutical manufacturers have sought to grow the market for a new drug through lower launch prices, co-payment coupons, and other promotional gimmicks in the early years, followed by aggressive price increases once the demand for the drug is established.

The most effective weapon that states and the private sector can use to reduce drug prices is to refuse to pay for overpriced drugs. That requires greater use of tools for evaluating the advantages of a new drug over existing treatments and demanding that the drug's price reflect its value. European countries do that well using independent agencies like the National Institute for Health and Care Excellence (NICE) in the United Kingdom. The Veteran's Administration has successfully used this approach to negotiate lower prices and exclude overpriced drugs from its National Formulary. Medicare and Medicaid continue to resist the use of comparative clinical evidence in drug purchasing decisions and insist on maintaining protected classes of drugs in which FDA approval guarantees access to a drug. The Patient-Centered Outcomes Research Institute (PCORI) was also expected to conduct rigorous patient-centered analyses of the merits of new drugs. Far more rigorous oversight by Congress is required to ensure that the funding that PCORI receives is used to evaluate existing medical treatments and provide payers with information that can be used to lower healthcare spending while assuring that patients utilize the most effective treatments.

In the private sector, institutions like the Institute for Clinical and Economic Review (ICER) and the Drug Effectiveness Review Project (DERP) have demonstrated the capacity to conduct rigorous but fair evaluations of the comparative value of new drugs. Insurance plans and large employers should contract with ICER and DERP to create regional or national formularies that exclude overpriced drugs or compel step therapy, prior authorization, and other means to restrict access to low-value drugs. Gross profit margins on drugs are enormous. Pharmaceutical manufacturers can make far more profit from lowering the price of a drug to expand its utilization than from maintaining a price that exceeds a drug's value.

3. INCREASING TAXPAYER RETURN FROM BIOMEDICAL RESEARCH FUNDING

The Bayh-Dole Act became law in 1980 when government investment in research was low, the discoveries by academics were broad concepts that required substantial additional investment to be translated into drugs, and the pharmaceutical industry was heavily investing in basic research. It was not foreseeable that NIH research grants, which now exceed $50 billion annually, would become the primary driver of drug discovery or that the pharmaceutical industry would become dependent on the government to produce its pipeline of new medicines. Nor would anyone have believed that drug prices would be so out of control that the government would routinely spend tens of billions annually in its Medicaid, Medicare, and military health programs for drugs that it also paid to discover.

In truth, it would be far less expensive for the government to pay the entire cost to develop a federally funded drug discovery than to pay the exorbitant prices charged by the pharmaceutical industry. That is precisely the government's approach to the defense industry, where it foots the bill for the entire cost of designing and developing a new weapons system but contracts out production under cost-plus contracts that limit profits to reasonable levels. Bayh-Dole must be amended or reinterpreted to define a more equitable public/private partnership arrangement. The government's contribution to discovering a new medicine should result in a lower price, a shorter monopoly period, or both. There must be a reasonable correlation between risk and reward. In the private sector, the party that finances a discovery retains a significant portion of the equity even though subsequent investors finance the commercial development of the discovery. When the government is the original funder, taxpayers' return on equity should be in the form of lower prices for the drug.

Bayh-Dole contains several provisions that recognize that the public should derive a financial benefit from inventions discovered with federal funds, but NIH and the other federal agencies that administer the law have treated those provisions as though they do not exist. For example, the law allows the government to march in and grant licenses to additional manufacturers to alleviate health and safety needs that are not being reasonably met by the exclusive licensee. NIH has repeatedly refused to exercise march-in rights that would allow generic manufacturers to produce a lower-cost drug because the price of a drug was too high.

Recently, the Biden Administration changed course and indicated that it is willing to develop a framework for exercising march-in rights in circumstances where a drug's price is too high. The National Institute of Standards and Technology (NIST), an agency within the Department of Commerce, has requested comment on its *Draft Interagency Guidance Framework for Considering the Exercise of March-In Rights* under the Bayh-Dole Act. This effort is not likely to have any meaningful impact. A secondary patent thicket developed with private funds covers most commercially important drugs. The government's march-in rights only apply to the patented inventions created with federal funds.

Bayh-Dole also grants the government a paid-up royalty-free license to practice any federally funded invention. In 2003, the Government Accountability Office ruled that federal agencies can contract with generic drug companies to manufacture low-cost generic drugs for government purposes. But for unexplained reasons, the government has refused to exercise this authority. Yet, exercising the Bayh-Dole license for the Xtandi patents would have saved Medicare billions of dollars on just one drug. The public is entitled to those savings.

An Executive Order requiring the government to utilize its Bayh-Dole licenses could save the government billions on the cost of drugs in government-sponsored health insurance plans such as Medicare and Medicaid without new legislation amending Bayh-Dole. That order should place authority for exercising the government's licenses in the hands of the Centers for Medicare & Medicaid Services (CMS), the VA, or some other agency responsible for negotiating drug prices. That agency should have the power to either authorize a generic manufacturer to produce a lower-cost generic version of a licensed drug for use and sale in government-sponsored health programs or to negotiate a lower price for the drug in exchange for refraining from doing so.

The Executive Order should also order the agency to exercise the government's immunity from claims for infringement of the thicket of secondary patents claiming a drug that were privately funded and are not subject to a Bayh-Dole license. Government procurement regulations established by the GAO in the late 1950s instruct agencies to disregard patents when acquiring drugs. Drug patent owners would be entitled to file claims against the government under 28 USC §1498 seeking reasonable compensation for infringement of secondary patents, but the recoveries will be trivial because those patents do not add significant value to the basic patent claiming the drug initially approved by the FDA which the government is entitled to practice under its royalty-free license.

The government is also losing billions in annual tax revenues from the sale of federally funded drugs because NIH has routinely waived the requirement in the Bayh-Dole Act that requires drugs discovered with federal funding to be manufactured in the United States unless it is not reasonably possible to do so. NIH has waived this provision more than one hundred times. Encouraging the offshore production of medicines not only reduces tax revenues; it also eliminates manufacturing jobs and endangers national security by increasing the risk of supply chain disruptions for essential medicines. An executive order can prevent future waivers, implement appropriate investigations to determine whether past waivers were justified, and roll back the improperly granted waivers.

Regulations promulgated under the Bayh-Dole Act also require the NIH to exercise oversight to ensure that the government receives all the patent licenses to which it is entitled and to monitor royalty collections. There is little reason to believe that NIH has effectively implemented this requirement. Published reports indicate that universities collect over $3 billion annually in royalties from federally funded discoveries. A significant share of these royalties may come from drugs purchased in Medicaid, Medicare, and other government-sponsored health insurance programs, even though the government owns a royalty-free license to use the patented invention for government purposes. Pharmaceutical manufacturers should pass that money to the government as an additional rebate rather than paying out a royalty where none is owed. An executive order could require an investigation into all current agency practices concerning federally funded inventions to ensure that the government receives all the benefits to which it is entitled under Bayh-Dole.

The failure of NIH and other agencies to properly implement and police Bayh-Dole is inexcusable and has cost the government billions of dollars. At a minimum, the government should ensure that it achieves savings on drug costs, tax revenues, and other benefits that offset the $50 billion annual cost of its biomedical research program. Pharmaceutical industry apologists will claim that the private sector won't invest in developing new drugs if the government reduces the potential profits. That is unlikely. The pharmaceutical industry is one of America's most profitable industries. To retain that profitability, it needs a pipeline of new drugs. Yet it no longer invests in the basic research required to maintain an independent pipeline, and it has become dependent on government-sponsored research to create a flow of new drug discoveries. Large pharmaceutical companies have become expensive middlemen in the drug development process and are no longer indispensable parties to that process. Unless they are willing to more reasonably share the fruits of those discoveries through lower prices and shorter monopolies, the wisest course of action may be for the government to fund the development of new drugs and have them manufactured under cost-plus contracts, leaving no role at all for the middlemen.

4. ASSURING THE AVAILABILITY OF LOW-COST GENERIC DRUGS

Chronic drug shortages, price gouging, and excessive prices caused by profiteering middlemen in the drug distribution process are all market failures that could have been avoided if some government agency had the responsibility and authority to monitor these important markets, spot emerging issues endangering price or supply, and take steps to intervene before a potential problem becomes a crises.

There are two main causes of drug shortages. One is the lack of an FDA-approved source for the finished product, and the other is the lack of a source for the active pharmaceutical ingredient. In either case, the FDA has access to the information required to anticipate the problem or to alleviate it when it occurs. It needs the organization and authority to do so.

The FDA maintains files identifying every approved Abbreviated New Drug Application (ANDA) and every discontinued ANDA. It also maintains Drug Master Files (DMFs), identifying present and former suppliers of every approved drug's active ingredient. Shortages caused by a lack of adequate capacity to manufacture a finished product usually arise because one or more manufacturers have discontinued the product or gone out of business, and the remaining producers have a production issue that has caused a voluntary or FDA-compelled shutdown or inadequate capacity. The FDA can avert the shutdown, seek to revive a discontinued ANDA, facilitate its transfer to an acceptable manufacturing facility, or facilitate importation from a foreign source. One of those possibilities will be the quickest way to end the shortage.

Supply chain shortages involving the active ingredient of a drug or an intermediary in its production have become more common. These pose a major long-term threat because domestic sources do not usually exist. China is a major source of these products, and dependence on China for an assured supply of essential medicines poses a national security risk. The US must develop the capacity to produce these ingredients domestically or in the Western Hemisphere. In the meantime, the FDA can seek to entice a manufacturer who has previously filed a DMF to go into production or facilitate the transfer of the technology necessary for producing the ingredient from a former DMF holder to a party capable of manufacturing it. As a last resort, the producer of the original branded product undoubtedly possesses some technology or ability to produce small quantities of that drug since it must have done so to produce the drug used in the initial clinical trials. The FDA must ensure that access to that know-how remains available for emergencies.

Regardless of the cause of a shortage, unless wholesalers, chain drug stores, and hospital buying groups commit to establishing profitable long-term relationships with potential new suppliers, no amount of effort by the FDA or any other federal agency to expedite generic approvals can successfully resolve a shortage. Potential new market entrants are not likely to assume any financial risk to serve the US market during shortages, knowing that drug purchasers have a history of driving prices down to unprofitable levels when supplies are adequate. The same type of consortium that enabled the creation of Civica Rx as a not-for-profit source of scarce generic drugs is necessary for those drugs that Civica Rx cannot produce on a timely basis. With such a consortium in place, the FDA can expedite approvals and inspections necessary to alleviate any shortage as quickly as possible.

Generic drug prices are also much higher than they should be because health plans have allowed Pharmacy Benefit Managers to earn excessive profits because of the lack of transparency about drug prices. That may now be changing. Widespread publicity regarding the corrupt practices of PBMs is generating new federal legislation designed to ensure that lower prices negotiated by PBMs benefit patients. At the same time, the prescription drug market is being disrupted by discount pharmacies that dispense drugs at a small markup over the actual acquisition cost of the pills, plus a reasonable dispensing fee.

It would make far more sense for federal and state governments to stop doing business with for-profit PBMs and use their own rather than trying to micromanage the PBM business. The Veterans Administration operates one of the most efficient PBMs in the country. It publishes a national formulary identifying the most clinically effective and cost-effective drugs for treating every condition. The formulary results from a rigorous analysis of published clinical studies comparing the effectiveness of drugs that treat the same condition. High-cost, low-value drugs-often heavily advertised and aggressively marketed to physicians are excluded from the formulary and are not routinely dispensed by VA doctors and pharmacies. Maintaining a formulary enables the VA to negotiate the lowest price in the US for every drug, and those prices are published.

If the VA PBM is good enough for veterans and active-duty service members, why isn't it the PBM of choice for Medicare and Medicaid? The VA pays pennies per pill for the most widely prescribed drugs. Billions could be saved annually if Medicare paid the VA price.

It makes no sense that the same pill dispensed from the same bottle can have many different prices depending on who is paying for the prescription. It's time to make drug prices transparent, eliminate rebate programs, and ensure that everyone, with or without insurance, pays the same price for the same prescription and that the least expensive clinically effective drug is dispensed.

The market value of Pfizer, adjusted for inflation, has grown eightfold from about $21 billion to $160 billion since 1984 when Hatch-Waxman was enacted. Merck's value is up twelve times from about $25 billion to $320 billion. During the same period, median family income adjusted for inflation has remained flat while per capita spending on medicines tripled to about $1500. Yet 90 percent of all prescriptions are filled with a low-cost generic drug. The bottom line is that pharmaceutical companies have gotten rich, and the cost of medicines is a financial burden for the average family despite the widespread availability of low-cost generic drugs. The most anyone can say is that the economic situation might be far worse for patients if pathways for the approval of generic drugs had not been created and most drugs had a perpetual monopoly. The great health economist Uwe Reinhardt hit the nail on the head when he said new drugs were priced the same way a bottle of water would be in the middle of the Sahara Desert.

Despite claims to the contrary, the Hatch-Waxman Act and the BPCIA have failed to establish a balance between incentives to encourage investment in discovering new medicines and the public's right to affordable medicines. The government has stood idly by while drug monopolies grew larger and drug prices soared. For decades, politicians have repeated the false mantra promoted by PhRMA—that the high cost of drugs is due to the high cost of research to discover them—while they simultaneously filled their campaign war chests with PhRMA money. The system is corrupt. For over forty years, I have tried to expose the problem and promote reasonable solutions. This book is the culmination of that effort. There is no doubt about the reasons for high drug prices and no shortage of reasonable solutions to the problem. But drug prices will remain high unless facts replace political contributions as the currency for making public policy.

About the Author

ALFRED ENGELBERG IS WIDELY REGARDED as the legal father of the modern generic drug industry for his work on the Hatch-Waxman Act, which created the framework for the explosive growth in generic drug use. Engelberg was a pioneer in challenging improperly granted drug patents that block generic competition on important medicines. He is the author of numerous articles on regulation of brand and generic competition, high prices on new drugs, the role of patent monopolies on drug price competition and innovation, drug shortages, and more. Al has degrees in Chemical Engineering (Drexel, 1961) and law (New York University, 1965) and has worked as a patent examiner, a patent agent for Exxon, a Justice Department trial lawyer, and a partner in an intellectual property law practice. He founded NYU's Engelberg Center on Innovation Law and Policy, is a fellow of the New York Academy of Medicine, and has been honored by NYU and others for his achievements in law and philanthropy.